# THE ENDURING NAVAHO

# THE ENDURING NAVAHO

BY LAURA GILPIN

UNIVERSITY OF TEXAS PRESS, AUSTIN & LONDON

By LAURA GILPIN

*The Pueblos: A Camera Chronicle*
*Temples in Yucatan*
*The Rio Grande: River of Destiny*

THIS BOOK IS PUBLISHED WITH THE ASSISTANCE OF THE
*Dan Danciger Publication Fund*

Library of Congress Catalog Card No. 68–55748

Type set by Service Typographers, Inc., Indianapolis, Indiana
Printed by The Meriden Gravure Company, Meriden, Connecticut
Color plates printed by The Steck Company, Austin, Texas
Bound by Universal Bookbindery, Inc., San Antonio, Texas

DEDICATED TO

ELIZABETH WARHAM FORSTER, R.N.

Dear Betsy:

This is as much your book as mine. Not only have you shared completely in the making of it, but also you have taught me to understand the Navaho People. Our association with the Navaho goes back to a vacation trip in the fall of 1930 when we were misdirected (by a white man) on the road from Kayenta to Chinle, Arizona, on the western side of the reservation, and got ourselves wonderfully lost, ending with an empty gasoline tank. How we laugh now over that experience. Yet how important it was, for it led you to a position as field nurse to the Navaho the following year.

I can see us now, sitting in the old Buick wondering what we should do. I, for some reason, thought I *had* to do something immediately. We were in the middle of a vast semidesert; visibility in every direction was fifty miles or more, but we saw nothing, not a distant hogan, nor a horse, nor a flock of sheep—just empty land. Leaving you to guard the car (from what I don't quite know!), I set forth on foot, with hope that another traveler might come along who would give you gasoline. How well I remember my thoughts as I trudged along, recalling every vivid tale I had ever heard of a similar experience. How mortified I was at having lost my way. I remember meeting a Navaho man and a little boy in a wagon, coming out of a wash. I tried to talk to them but they spoke no English. I pointed in the direction of Chinle, indicating that I would pay them to take me there, but the man shook his head; then, reaching for something under a canvas in the wagon bed, he handed me three cool, delicious peaches. Finally, after an emotionally stimulated walk of two and one half hours, I reached Frazier's trading post. The trader was away, but his understanding wife took me and the needed gasoline back to you and the car, a distance of more than ten miles. I remember imagining how worried you must have been over my long absence. Never will I forget topping a gentle rise in the undulating desert and seeing the lonely car completely surrounded by *Navaho Indians*, like a swarm of bees about a honeysuckle. When we arrived, there you were in the midst of the gathering, happily playing cards with your visitors! Your ensuing tale of how the Navaho had arrived, two or three at a time, seemingly from nowhere, to find out what the trouble was and to offer help, both surprised and interested me.

I recall my concern of a year later, when you told me you were accepting a position as field nurse to the Navaho, sponsored by a private organization. I wondered where and how you would live, what your work would consist of, whom you would have to help you. Later when I came to visit, I found you in snug though primitive quarters. As I listened to tales of your experiences, I, too, became interested in these people, impressed by their rugged character and their mode of life. From time to time my visits revealed the work you were doing, your understanding, your patience, your kindness, and your generosity, for you literally gave of your substance as well as your knowledge and nursing skill. I saw the response of the Navaho People to your attitude toward them, your willingness to go anywhere at any time when a call came for help. I know, too, the lives you saved and the succor you gave.

When the depression came and there were no more funds for the continuation of your work, you had to leave. I helped you pack and move. I can relive that final morning when six of your best friends arrived, watching our every act, then suddenly, solemnly, and without warning, stood, bowed their heads, and wept in unison.

During the past eighteen years, together we have hunted for old friends after a lapse of nearly thirty years, finding many, making many new ones, and exploring nearly the whole of the reservation. I have watched old friends turn to you for medical aid the moment they saw your face. What fun we have had evolving this book. Your help when I was after difficult pictures, your sound criticism, and your encouragement, finally, have brought the book to completion. As a tribute to our long and happy friendship, this is your book.

# PREFACE

Within the boundaries of their 25,000-square-mile reservation, more than 100,000 Navaho People, the largest tribe of Indians in North America, are striving for existence on a land not productive enough to sustain their increasing population. They are striving not only to exist, but also to meet an encroaching way of life with which they are, in a large measure, unfamiliar. It is within the last thirty years that the Navaho have been faced with this growing necessity for change, a change so great for them, that we can scarcely comprehend it. Their traditional mode of living—simple, carefree, undisturbed by the great pressures of our complex civilization—is being changed through their adaptation to an utterly alien existence.

In past years nature provided sufficient pasture for the Navaho flocks and sufficient arable land for their simple farming, while the trading posts offered a market for their products. Today the Navaho find themselves with a population more than three times greater than their land can support. Thirty years ago they felt the white man far away, save for those few with whom they traded, but today they are surrounded by a constantly growing white population. Navaholand is no longer the faraway wild country of the Southwest. This encroaching pressure is sharply felt, and the Navaho are rising to meet it. Thirty years ago many were reluctant to go to the reservation schools; they were shy and diffident about learning the ways of our people. Today, they are clamoring for education, for there are many more children who want to go to school than there are schools or teachers to fill this demand.

It has been my privilege to observe some of the old life and much of the transition to the new. It has been intensely interesting, often heartbreaking, sometimes amusing, and in general has filled me with admiration for these people. Photography is essentially the medium for recording and interpreting such change. There is no pretense here of a scientific or an ethnologic approach, but all factual statements have been checked with some of our leading scientists and, finally, with the Navaho People themselves.

There are many books about the Navaho, books by anthropologists, physicians, psychologists, and experienced laymen. Many of the authors have far greater knowledge of the Navaho than I. My endeavor has been to create a visual image of these people, together with an explanatory text. As pictures and ideas accumulated, they fell into four categories; therefore, it seemed quite in keeping with Navaho tradition to divide this book into four parts. First, "The Navaho World," with its geographic conception and mythology; second, "The Way of the People," depicting their mode of life and their activities; third, "The Coming Way," denoting the present transition from the old ways to the new; and fourth, "The Enduring Way," the way of Navaho belief, which binds the People together through their traditional ceremonialism.

Some of these pictures were made more than thirty years ago, most of them between 1950 and 1965 when the photographic work was completed. I am well aware of many gaps, but it is my hope that these pages will stir an understanding of this energetic tribe, and awaken an interest in its imaginative and poetic background.

I have been fortunate indeed in the friends I have made and the co-operation I have received from interested Navaho People. This, therefore, is an interpretation of a wonderful people just as I have found them, a people having great pride, dignity, and ability who deserve our sincere respect.

Laura Gilpin

*Santa Fe, New Mexico*

# ACKNOWLEDGMENTS

So many people have helped in one way or another over the many years this book has been in the making, that it would be a long list indeed to name them all. To the following I am deeply grateful for their help and criticism.

To the many Navaho People who have willingly helped in allowing me to make these photographs and who helped in other ways, and to the following friends who have given specific help:

| | |
|---|---|
| Sam Ahkeah | Ned Hatathli |
| Maria Teba Bia | Maurice McCabe |
| Sam Day III | Annie Wauneka |

To Mr. and Mrs. Nathaniel A. Owings, whose interest in this book has led them to the generous act of providing nine of the color plates.

To John Adair, for checking the section on silversmithing; to E. Boyd, for her general appraisal; to David Brugge, archaeologist for the Navaho Tribe; to Ann Nolan Clark, for her sound criticism in writing; to Virginia Comer, for her help in general; to Dr. Alfred E. Dittert, Jr., curator in charge, Research Division of the Museum of New Mexico, for taking me to the site of the petroglyphs; to Alison Dodge, with the Navajo Sheep Breeding Laboratory; to Dr. Bertha Dutton, director of the Museum of Navaho Ceremonial Art, for her permission to photograph ceremonial objects; to Irene Emery, of the Textile Museum of Washington, D.C., for checking the section on weaving; to Elspeth Eubank, teacher at the Navajo Mountain School, for introducing me to Navaho People in her region; to Dr. Marion Hotopp, for help with the section on public health; to Mary Blue Huey, for her excellent map; to the Indian Arts Fund and the School of American Research, for permission to photograph many objects in their joint collections; to David J. and Courtney Jones, for their valuable help; to Marjorie F. Lambert, curator, Research Division of the Museum of New Mexico, for her appraisal of the entire work; to the late Dorothea Lange, photographer, who gave great encouragement to this project; to Martin Link, director of the Navajo Museum, Window Rock, Arizona; to Robert Measeles, Bureau of Indian Affairs, for his help in securing information about the Checkerboard Area; to Mabel Morrow, long with the Education Division of the Bureau of Indian Affairs, for her careful checking of the whole craft section; to staff members of the National Park Service, for their help at many locations; to Cornelia G. Thompson, for permitting me to photograph many pieces from her Navaho silver collection; to Betty Toulouse, for her excellent proof reading; to Virginia von Schrenk, for her typing of the manuscript; to the late Richard Van Valkenburgh, for his interest and help; and to Robert W. Young, of the Bureau of Indian Affairs, for his help on the Navaho language and pronunciation guide.

To the following traders:

| | |
|---|---|
| The late Bruce Bernard | Shiprock |
| Sam Day III | Pine Springs |
| Charles Dickens | Shiprock |
| Rubin Hefflin | Shonto |
| The late Roman Hubbell | Ganado |
| Troy Kennedy | Red Rock |
| Sally and William Lippincott | Wide Ruins |
| The late "Cozy" McSparron | Chinle |
| Carlos Stolworthy | Red Rock |
| Don Watson | Cortez |

And to several anonymous friends who lent a helping hand along the way.

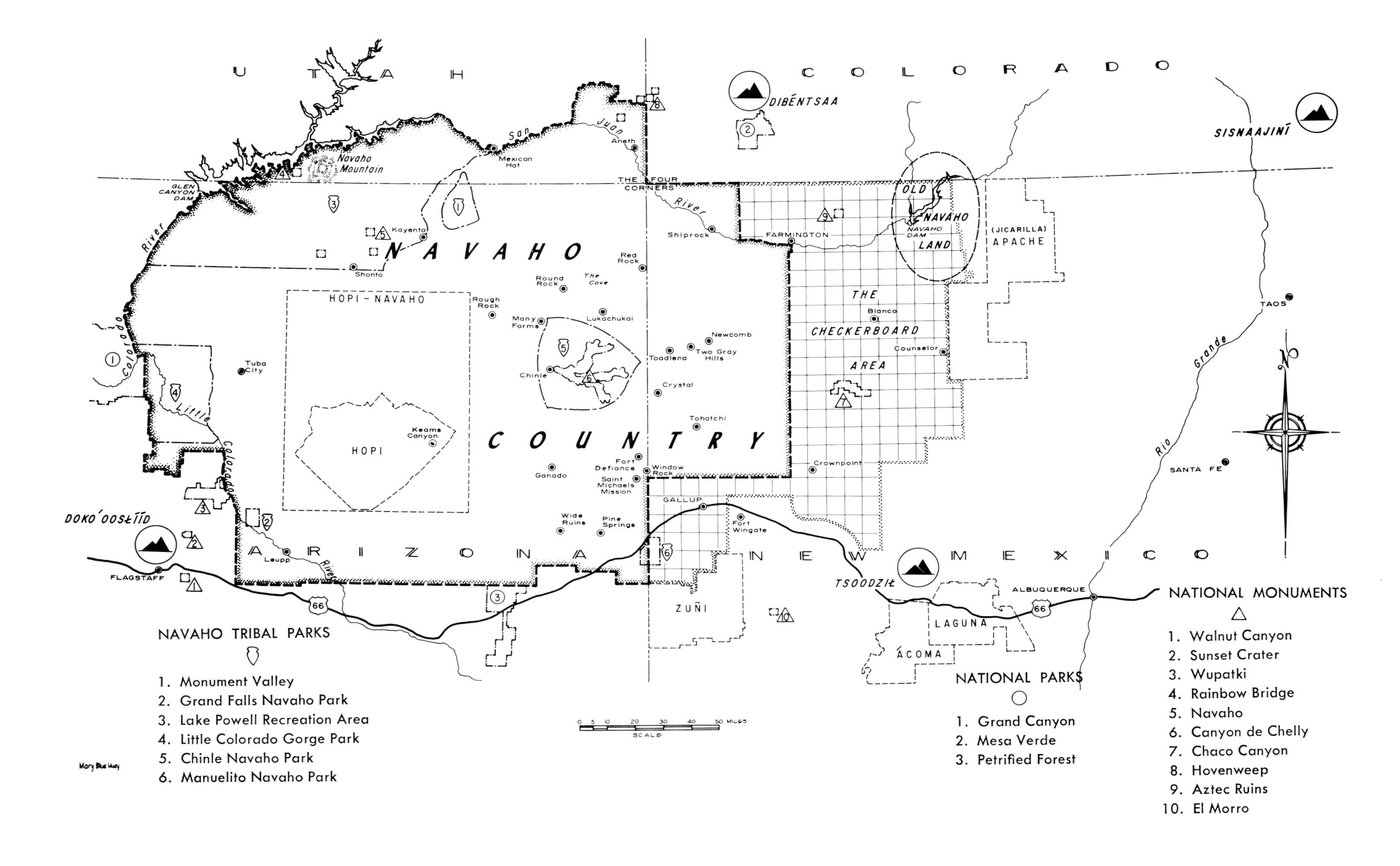
UTAH
COLORADO
ARIZONA
NEW MEXICO
NAVAHO COUNTRY
DIBÉNTSAA
SISNAAJINÍ
DOKO'OOSŁÍÍD
TSOODZIŁ
THE CHECKERBOARD AREA
OLD NAVAHO LAND
NAVAHO DAM
(JICARILLA) APACHE
HOPI-NAVAHO
HOPI
ZUÑI
LAGUNA
ÁCOMA
GLEN CANYON DAM
Navaho Mountain
San Juan River
Colorado River
Little Colorado River
Rio Grande
THE FOUR CORNERS
Mexican Hat
Aneth
Kayenta
Shonto
Tuba City
Keams Canyon
Rough Rock
Round Rock
The Cove
Red Rock
Many Farms
Lukachukai
Chinle
Shiprock
FARMINGTON
Blanca
Counselor
Newcomb
Two Gray Hills
Toadlena
Crystal
Tohatchi
Crownpoint
Fort Defiance
Window Rock
Saint Michaels Mission
Ganado
Wide Ruins
Pine Springs
GALLUP
Fort Wingate
Leupp
FLAGSTAFF
ALBUQUERQUE
SANTA FE
TAOS
66
NAVAHO TRIBAL PARKS
1. Monument Valley
2. Grand Falls Navaho Park
3. Lake Powell Recreation Area
4. Little Colorado Gorge Park
5. Chinle Navaho Park
6. Manuelito Navaho Park
NATIONAL PARKS
1. Grand Canyon
2. Mesa Verde
3. Petrified Forest
NATIONAL MONUMENTS
1. Walnut Canyon
2. Sunset Crater
3. Wupatki
4. Rainbow Bridge
5. Navaho
6. Canyon de Chelly
7. Chaco Canyon
8. Hovenweep
9. Aztec Ruins
10. El Morro
0 5 10 20 30 40 50 MILES
SCALE
Mary Blue Huey

# CONTENTS

# THE ENDURING NAVAHO

# PART I

# THE NAVAHO WORLD

# THE CREATION STORY

To understand the Navaho People, even in small measure, it is essential to know at least some part of their symbolic ritual. That they have so rich a tradition comes as a surprise to those unfamiliar with their background. The Navaho have retained their culture through centuries without the use of written language, without centers of education, and without a religious head, for there is no such office—it simply exists in every person, in every family, in every part of their land. As the legends, the chants, and the symbolism are myriad, and as knowledge of these must be handed down by word of mouth or they will perish, Navaho capacity for memory has become very great. There is always a medicine man who carries on these beliefs, who conducts the ceremonies, who teaches others. The Creation Story, as its title indicates, contains the roots of this symbolism, and signifies Navaho relation to all of nature. Like our Old Testament, the Navaho story contains a flood, expulsion from one world to another, and, throughout, a strong suggestion of evolution.

Beginning with Dr. Washington Matthews, an Army surgeon stationed at Fort Wingate in the 1880's, and followed by a number of students and anthropologists who gathered their information from many medicine men, this legend has been recorded, and, though there are variations, the basic characters are similar. From the Story has come the Blessingway Ceremony—the ceremonial most sacred to the Navaho People—and also the great variety of symbolic uses of plants and animals, birds and insects, colors and substances. The sacred number *four* permeates Navaho thinking. There are the four directions, the four seasons, and the four colors and substances associated with the four sacred mountains: white and white shell indicate the East; blue and turquoise, the South;

yellow and coral or abalone, the West; black and jet, the North. In most rituals there are four songs and multiples thereof, as well as many other symbolic uses of four.

The Navaho believe that the People came from lower worlds, passing through four of them (some say twelve) to emerge into this present Fifth World. Early Navaho concept, like that of all primitive peoples, was that the world was flat, that the sky was supported by supernatural beings, that the sun came in the morning and left at night, and that the moon and stars were hung in the sky to be seen after the sun had departed. They believe that the next world is the world of the spirit, beyond which is a world where everything merges into the cosmos. Their only concern, however, is with this present life in the Fifth World.

The Story tells of life beginning in a lower world, the First World, where it was predestined that the prototypes of living creatures, as well as inanimate elements, would come into being. Here began the duality of life, male and female. There were twelve kinds of people inhabiting this First World, which was dark, and though they are spoken of as people, they were insects as we know them. There were Dark Ants—Red Ants—Dragon Flies—Yellow Beetles—Stone Carrier Beetles—Dung Beetles—Hard Beetles—Black Beetles—Bats—White Faced Beetles—Locusts—and White Locusts. There were oceans far off in each direction, and in each ocean a chief or deity. The People quarreled among themselves and the chiefs told them they must go elsewhere.

Entering a hole in the East, the People emerged into the Second World. Here they found the Bird People, with whom they made friends. They sent out their couriers, Locust and White Locust, to explore the land, but though they reached the edge of the world, they found only bare ground. After a while there was more quarreling, and the Bird People told them they must go away.

Once more they flew upward and, finding a cleft in the sky, they found their way into the Third World. Again the couriers went out to explore and again found bare land, except for a great river flowing to the East. This was the female river, and flowing into it was the male river, thus symbolizing generation. Grasshopper People lived in the Third World and the People mingled with them, requesting that they might live as one tribe. But once again there was quarreling, and once more they were expelled. The People flew upward in wide circles but found the sky hard and smooth. As they searched for an exit, a red head emerged from the sky. It was the Red Wind, who told them to fly to the West. Here they found a spiral passage made by the Wind, and flying up through it they reached the Fourth World. Four Grasshopper People went with them, one white, one blue, one yellow, and one black, and to this day the People have grasshoppers of these colors.

When the People entered the Fourth World, they saw four great snow-covered mountains on the far horizon of each direction. Once again the couriers went out to explore. To the East they found no sign of life, to the South they saw tracks of the deer and the turkey, and to the West again no sign of life. But when they returned from the North, the couriers told of finding a race of strange men, who cut their hair square in front, who lived in houses on the ground, and who cultivated fields. The following day, two of these strangers—the Kiis'aanii (the Pueblo People)—came to the exiles' camp and later guided them to a river. The water was red, and the Kiis'aanii told the People that they must not cross the river on foot or their feet would be injured. The Kiis'aanii showed the People a square raft made of logs—a white pine, a blue spruce, a yellow pine, and a black spruce. The People crossed the river to visit the homes of these new friends, who gave them corn and pumpkins to eat. As this land had neither rain nor snow, the crops were raised by irrigation.

Late in the autumn the People heard the sound of a distant voice calling. It came from the East. Three times more they heard the voice, each time nearer than before. At last four mysterious beings appeared. They were White Body, Blue Body, Yellow Body, and Black Body. These beings made signs to the People but did not speak, and after they had gone the People wondered what these signs meant. Three times the gods visited them but still did not talk. On the fourth day Black Body stayed after the others had gone, and spoke to the People in their own language:

You do not understand the signs the gods make to you. I will tell you what they mean. The gods wish to make more people, but they want the forms of these people to be like themselves. You have bodies like theirs, but you have the teeth, the feet, and the claws of insects. The new people will have hands and feet like ours. Have yourselves well cleansed when we return, which will be in twelve days.

On the morning of the twelfth day, the People washed themselves thoroughly, the women drying themselves with yellow corn meal, the men with white corn meal. Soon they heard the call of the gods shouted four times, each time nearer than before, and after the fourth call the gods appeared. Blue Body and Black Body each carried a sacred buckskin. White Body carried two ears of corn, one white and one yellow, each perfect with grains to the tip. One buckskin was laid on the ground with the head to the West. On it they placed the two ears of corn with the tips to the East. Under the white ear they put a feather from the white eagle, and under the yellow ear, a feather from the yellow eagle. Over all they spread the other buckskin.

The gods told the People to stand away to allow the Winds to enter. The White Wind blew from the East and the Yellow Wind from the West, blowing between the buckskins. While the Winds were blowing, eight Mirage People came, walking around the skins four times. While they walked, the People saw the feathers move. When the Mirage People had completed their fourth round, the upper skin was lifted. A man and a woman lay where the ears of corn had been; the white ear had been changed into a man, the yellow ear into a woman, and the Winds had given them life. It is the wind coming out of our mouths that gives us life—when it stops, we die. In the skin at the tips of our fingers we can see the trail of the Winds. Thus the gods created First Man and First Woman.

The first children born to First Man and First Woman were hermaphrodite twins. Then more twins were born. After the birth of the last pair, the gods took First Man and First Woman away to the East Mountain and kept them there four days. When they returned, all the children were taken to the same place. After they had all made the journey to the Sacred Mountain, they occasionally wore masks, and when this happened they prayed for all good things, for rain and abundant crops.

The children of First Man and First Woman married among the Mirage People, and they in turn bore many children. Some of their offspring married among the Kiis'aanii and the People from the lower worlds, and soon there were many people, with First Man as their chief.

The People from the Third World had been in the Fourth World for eight years when one day they saw the Sky stooping down and the Earth rising to meet it. From the point of contact there sprang from the Earth, Coyote and Badger, children of the Sky. Coyote, the elder, came and skulked around the People, but Badger went down the hole that led to the lower world and was rarely seen.

One day, following a feast of deer meat, First Woman made a remark which made her husband angry and they had a quarrel. The next morning First Man called all the men together, telling them what his wife had said—that the women thought they could get along without the men. "Let us leave them," he said, "and see if they can till the fields and hunt game, and let us take the Kiis'aanii with us." So they crossed the river on the raft taking with them the things they had made. The Kiis'aanii went too, but they took their wives with them.

During the first year all went well, the women had plenty of food, and they sang and had a merry time. As the men had to start new fields, they did not have much to eat. The second year the women did not do so well, while the men increased their fields and crops. In the third year the women did still less well, and the men better by far. In the fourth year the women had little to eat and the men much more than they needed.

First Man began to think about what he had done and that the race might perish. He sent a messenger to ask First Woman if she still thought she could live alone. The answer came back that the women could not live without their husbands. Therefore, amidst great rejoicing, the women were brought across the river on the raft. It was soon discovered that three were missing, a woman and her two daughters. After nightfall the voices of the missing ones were heard begging to be ferried across, but they were told to wait until morning. The mother could not wait and swam across, but the daughters disappeared. For three days and nights the People heard nothing of the missing ones.

On the morning of the fourth day the call of the gods was heard, and after the fourth call White Body appeared holding up two fingers and pointing to the river. White Body went away but soon returned with Blue Body, each carrying a bowl, one white and one blue. They put the bowls on the water, spinning them as they did so, and the water parted beneath the bowls, giving entrance to a house with four rooms, one in each direction. The mother of the missing girls and her husband entered the house, Coyote following them, and, finding the first three rooms empty, they entered the fourth room, to the north. Here they saw Water Monster, with two of his children, and sitting beside him were their own two daughters. The man and woman demanded their daughters, and, as Water Monster said nothing, they took them and went away. While no one was looking, Coyote slyly stole the children of the Water Monster, hiding them under his robe. No one noticed this, for Coyote always wore his robe folded around himself.

The next day the People were surprised to see all sorts of game running past them, going from East to West. This went on for three days, and on the morning of the fourth day they saw a strange gleam after the white light rose in the East. They sent the Locust Couriers to see what it was. They returned to say that there was a vast flood approaching from the East. The People and the Kiis'aanii assembled, bemoaning their fate and knowing not what to do. They climbed a hill to hold a council. Then they saw two men drawing near; one was old and had grey hair, the other was young. They passed right through the crowd without speaking and sat down on top of the hill, the young man in front, the old man behind him, and Locust behind them both, and they all turned and faced the East. The old man took seven bags from his robe, telling the People that he had bits of earth from the Seven Sacred Mountains. The People asked him if he could help them, and he replied that perhaps his son could, but the People must face the West, for they must not see him at his work.

Soon the People were called and they saw the sacred earth spread out on the ground. Planted in it were four reeds with four joints, and, as they watched, the roots spread out, going into the earth, and the reeds joined into one, growing rapidly; in the eastern side of the big reed was a great hole. The young man told the People to enter, and when they were all in, the hole closed behind them and they heard the splashing of the waters as the flood came near. Turkey was the last to enter the reed and his tail got wet with the foam from the flood, and that is why Turkey has white tips to his tail feathers.

As the People climbed inside the reed it soon began to sway, but Black Body blew a great breath through the top of the reed and a black cloud formed around the top, holding it steady. The reed grew higher as the People climbed, and again it began to sway. Black Body took a plume from his headband and stuck it through the top of the reed, fastening it to the sky. And that is why the reed now always carries a plume. The People sent Locust up to find a hole in the sky, and finding a small opening he passed through it into the upper world, coming out on an island in the middle of a lake. But the hole was too small for the People to get through, so they sent Badger to dig it out. When Badger returned, his legs were all covered with mud and that is why the legs of badgers have been black ever since.

Then First Man and First Woman led the way and they all emerged to the surface of this, the Fifth World. On the fourth day, someone looked down through the hole and saw the water rushing up. First Man called a council and, pointing to Coyote, said that something was wrong about Coyote, for he never took off his robe. The People searched Coyote and two strange objects fell to the ground. These were the children of the Water Monster whom Coyote had stolen from under the river. The People threw the children into the hole and at once the water subsided.

On the fifth night one of the hermaphrodite twins stopped breathing and all the People wondered what had become of her breath; they hunted for it everywhere. While the People were hunting for the lost breath, two men looked down the hole of emergence, and there they saw the hermaphrodite sitting on a rock combing her hair. They told the People what they had seen, but on the fourth day both men died, and ever since the People have feared to look upon the dead.

Now the Kiis'aanii were camped some little distance from the others, and one of the People found that they had brought an ear of corn with them from the lower world. Some People wanted to take this away from the Kiis'aanii, while others said that that would be wrong, but some young men went to demand the corn, and angry words followed. But the friendly Kiis'aanii offered to break the ear in two and give the People their choice of the pieces. While the young men were considering which piece to take, Coyote grabbed the

tip and ran away with it, leaving the butt end for the Kiis'aanii, and that is why the Pueblo People have always had better corn than the Navaho. After the angry words, the Kiis'aanii moved away from the People, which is why they and the Navaho live apart today.

Then First Man and First Woman, Black Body and Blue Body built seven sacred mountains in the Fifth World, using the earth brought from the lower world. And the four great mountains were Sisnaajiní to the East, Tsoodził to the South, Doko'oosłíí́d to the West, and Dibéntsaa to the North. Within these boundaries were the three lesser mountains, Ch'óół'į́'í, Dził ná'óodiłii, and Naatsis'áán. These are still the sacred mountains of the Dinéh, the Navaho People.[1]

But times were bad and there were many Enemy Monsters who killed and ate people. One day First Man was standing on Dził ná'óodiłii, and looking to the East he saw a rain cloud resting on Ch'óół'į́'í. Each day it enveloped the mountain more and more, and on the fourth day it completely covered it. He told First Woman that something unusual was happening, and set forth to see what it was, singing a Blessing Song as he went.

When First Man reached Ch'óół'į́'í, he heard a baby cry; he found the baby lying with its head toward

[1] The contemporary locations of the sacred mountains are *Sisnaajiní*, Mount Blanca, San Luis Valley, Colorado; *Tsoodził*, Mount Taylor, north of Laguna, New Mexico; *Doko'oosłíí́d*, the San Francisco Peaks, near Flagstaff, Arizona; *Dibéntsaa*, Mount Hesperus, La Plata Mountains, Colorado; *Ch'óół'į́'í*, Gobernador Knob, in Old Navaholand, southeast of the reservoir; *Dził ná'óodiłii*, Huerfano Mesa, south of Farmington, New Mexico; and *Naatsis'áán*, Navaho Mountain, southeastern Utah.

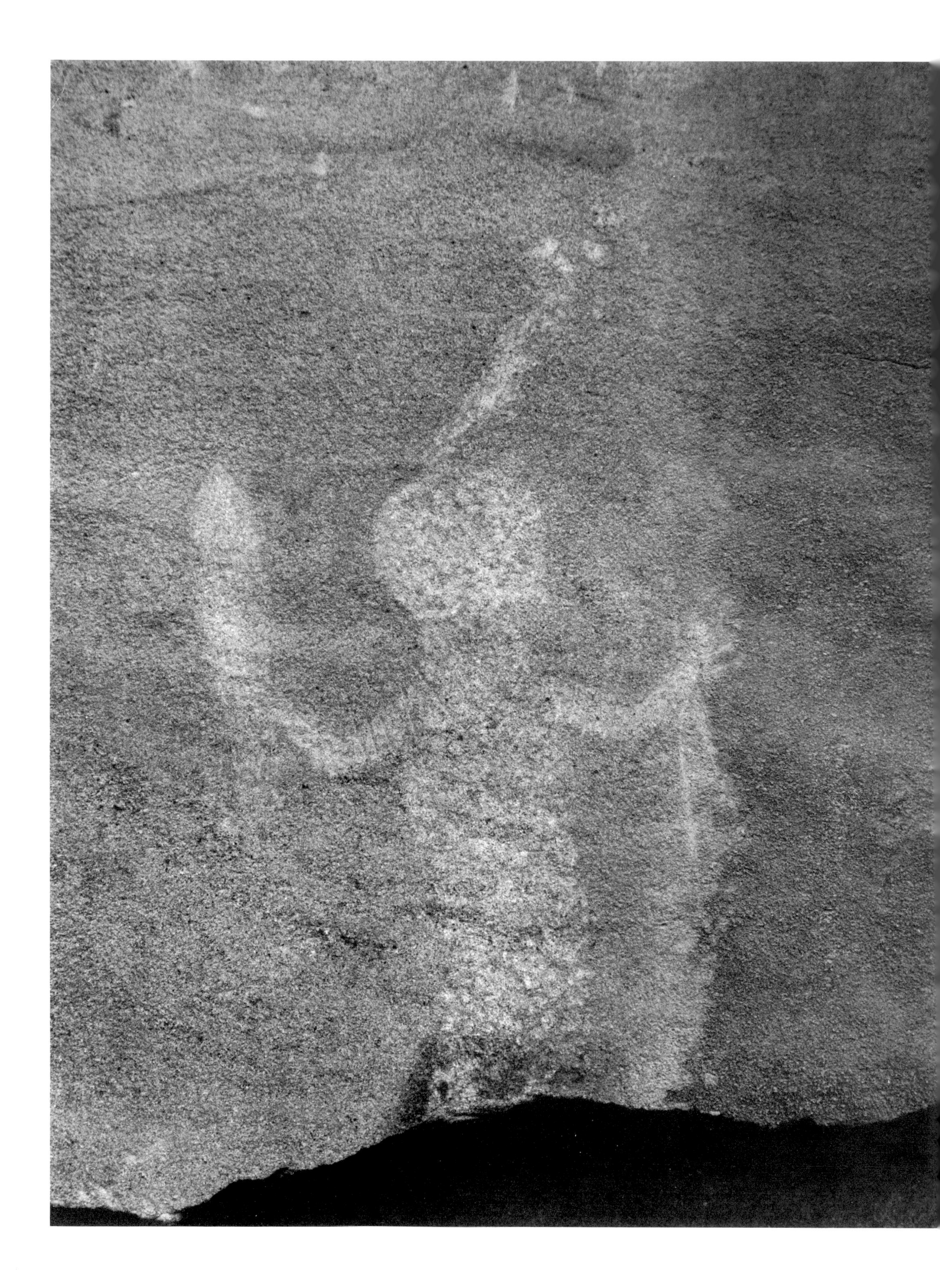

the West. Its cradle was made of two short rainbows; over the baby's chest and feet lay the red beams of the rising sun; arched over its face was another short rainbow. Four blankets covered the baby: one was black, one was blue, one was yellow, and the fourth was a white cloud. Along both sides were rows of loops made of lightning, and, through these, sunbeams were laced back and forth. As First Man did not know what to do with the fastenings, he took the baby back to Dził ná'oodilii to First Woman, telling her where he had found the baby in the rain and darkness. Soon they heard the call of Talking God, and then the call of House God, as the gods approached. Talking God clapped his hands over his mouth saying that something important had happened, for the baby was what the Holy People had been wishing for. Talking God placed the cradle on the ground and, with one pull of the strings, freed the lacings.

"This is my daughter," First Woman said, and First Man said the same. Days passed which were the same as years, and when two days had passed, the baby sat up, and in four days she walked. Then she was dressed in white shell. On the tenth day she was named White Shell Woman (she was also called Changing Woman), and thus she was brought by the Holy People to become, perhaps, the most pre-eminent of the supernatural beings, for she symbolizes fertility, and regeneration, and the bringing of all green things to life year after year.

Just below the junction of the San Juan and the Pine rivers in north central New Mexico, where the new Navajo Dam is now creating a large reservoir, there was a meadow on the eastern side of the San Juan. Along one side of the meadow was a cliff of reddish sandstone, and etched into the façade was a series of petroglyphs, chipped out of the rock with obsidian tools centuries ago.

Here also were the remnants of weatherworn rock paintings of the Twin Hero Gods (The Twin War Gods), sons of Changing Woman and the Sun, who slew the Enemy Monsters on this earth so that the Dinéh might safely live here. The story relates how a ray of light from the Sun passed through drops of water from a waterfall, impregnating Changing Woman. When the twins were born, one was called Monster Slayer, the other, Child-of-the-Water.

Nearby, on this sheer slab of rock was a petroglyph with all the attributes of Changing Woman herself: in one hand she holds an ear of corn; in the other, a corn tassel containing pollen; around her neck is the rainbow necklace, made from the sacred stones from the four sacred mountains—white shell, turquoise, coral, and jet.

Now these ancient pictures are submerged beneath the waters of the reservoir; but surely the spirit of Changing Woman will bless this water as it goes forth onto the dry and barren land, fulfilling her mission of renewal, and bringing new crops and a richer life to many of the Dinéh.

### *Maize*

The domestication and hybridization of maize, or corn, has been perhaps the most important achievement of the American Indian, giving the Western

Hemisphere its most stable food. For many years scientists have searched for the true ancestor of corn such as was found in the Americas at the time of the arrival of the first European explorers. A good many years ago scientists found two wild grasses related to corn, but not true corn itself. Recently the great antiquity of corn was proved with the finding of corn pollen in drilled cores taken from strata at the bottom of the lake site on which Mexico City now stands. These pollen grains are estimated to be eighty thousand years old.

Following this discovery a systematic search has been under way since 1960, headed by Dr. Richard MacNeish of Canada[2] and his associates. Some previous findings in New Mexico and northern Mexico had produced corncobs which, when tested by the remarkable Carbon-14 method of dating substances, were approximately five thousand years old. Now, after four years of excavation and research, cave sites in the valley of Tehuacan, south of Mexico City, have yielded the final evidence of the true corn plant and the proof of its domestication and hybridization. In these caves, beneath twenty-eight layers of human occupation, corncobs from the true wild plant were found dating back to 5000 B.C. Each era of occupation left its evidence: in later levels dating about 4000 B.C., cobs from early domesticated corn were found; then an early hybrid variety dating 3000 B.C.; and finally, dating 1000 B.C., cobs from modern corn, such as that found in a growing state by the European explorers.

Dr. MacNeish's team, which included archaeologists, botanists, and scientists of other related subjects, has found that this hybridization was achieved with the use of the wild corn plant itself and the two related wild grasses, teosinte and tripsacum, thus producing the early corn of some three thousand years ago.

Of the three major cereals of the world—wheat in Africa spreading to Europe, rice in Asia, and corn in the Americas—it is only corn, modern corn, that is, which cannot perpetuate itself in a wild state. With its seeds tightly wrapped in sheaths, corn needs man's help to disperse the seeds so that they may grow. As domestication and hybridization of this plant increased, following the early uses of irrigation, knowledge of its cultivation spread from one Indian group to another and on to the far regions of both Americas where the plant could grow, and where it was found in its fully developed state by the first Europeans who set foot in the Western Hemisphere.

This food, so vital to existence for many centuries, has always been held sacred by Indian peoples. In the Southwest, corn is the symbol of the great dance dramas of the Pueblo People. To the Navaho, it is the symbolic emblem of life itself. It is treasured and revered. Every medicine man carries pouches of sacred corn pollen to be used in all rituals: in the Blessingway Ceremony; in the great ceremonials; in the blessing of hogans. Sacred corn mush is eaten simultaneously from the wedding basket by every Navaho bride and groom.

*The Four Sacred Mountains*

While I was reading the Creation Story, my thoughts traveled to the four sacred mountains bordering the Navaho World. It was then, I think, that it occurred to me to illustrate this beautiful story with photographs of these mountains from the air. To do this two flights were necessary, the first for Sisnaajiní, Sacred Mountain of the East, and the second, longer, flight for the other three. Perhaps it is my love for landscape and geography that makes me want to fly. From the air one can see so clearly the great structures of the earth's surface, the different kinds of mountains, the sweep of contours, the age-old erosions. In the air one becomes detached and the mind goes deep into the past, thinking of Time in depth.

In a small chartered plane, my pilot and I left Santa Fe early one morning with the picture of Sisnaajiní as our goal. As we circled to gain altitude, the form of the Sandia Mountain fault, to the south of us, became more distinct in structure with its rising eastern slope and the sheer, abrupt western face. In a cave high in this western wall, the earliest evidence of human life in this area has been found, remnants of migrants who lived here fifteen thousand years ago—so old is the history of our Southwest. The present theory is that these ancient primitives came to North America from Mongolia via Bering Strait, moving slowly southward over a period of centuries.

We headed north following the Rio Grande, seeing clearly the canyons cut by the river through the volcanic slopes of the Pajarito Plateau. As we crossed

[2] Dr. Richard MacNeish, "The Origins of New World Civilization," *Scientific American*, 211, No. 5 (November, 1964), 29–37.

*Sisnaajiní (Mount Blanca), Sacred Mountain of the East.*

into southern Colorado the superb mountain mass of Sisnaajiní grew more impressive as we neared. Beneath us the southern end of the San Luis Valley looked barren and uninhabited. Here once was an abundance of game—elk and antelope, deer and bison—and here the ancient Navaho came to hunt, seeing always their sacred mountain before them. To the West, over the continental divide, the new Navajo Dam has now been completed at the confluence of the San Juan and the Pine rivers. Just above the dam site during the field seasons of 1959, 1960, and 1961, the salvage archaeology project of the Museum of New Mexico uncovered more comprehensive data of the early whereabouts of the Navaho and their Apache cousins. These sites, farther north than excavations made some years ago by other archaeologists, have extended the area known as Old Navaholand. These recent unearthings have revealed simple, crude hogans (Navaho houses) dating from about the middle of the sixteenth century. This date seems to indicate that the Navaho may well have been the last migration to reach the Southwest. Whence and how they came has yet to be determined.

The Spanish colonists who arrived in New Mexico in 1598 came in contact with many Indian groups. During the years that followed, they wrote often of the Apaches, usually designating which Apache group, for there must have been several at that time, all speaking the Athabascan language. In the chronicle of Fray Gerónimo de Zárate Salmerón, written in 1626, he speaks of the "Apaches de Návahúu," who were living in a small pueblo on the Pajarito Plateau not far from Santa Fe. *Návahúu* is a Tewa Indian word meaning "cultivated-field-arroyo" and is the word from which *Navaho* is doubtless derived.[3] The Navaho learned the rudiments of agriculture from Pueblo Indians with whom they came in contact, for archaeologists working in the Old Navaholand areas have found both Pueblo and Navaho structures in close proximity to one another. In these Navaho excavations the archaeologists found remnants of corn, squash, and bean seed.

Thinking always of the Navaho, where they came from and how they traveled, we could see from the air that the distance from Old Navaholand to Sisnaajiní is not great, and, though there are mountains in between, there are passes through which travelers can find a way, and the Navaho doubtless came into the valley to hunt. Because of its severance by a wide, low pass, Sisnaajiní appears to be a mountain by itself and is a natural landmark—Sisnaajiní, Navaho Sacred Mountain of the East.

Following plans for a longer flight to photograph the Sacred Mountains of the South, West, and North, we left Santa Fe shortly after daylight on an early spring morning. We headed west toward the low end of the Jemez Range, beyond which stretches the expanse of the Navaho Reservation. Crossing the Rio Grande, we saw below us on the river's western bank the skeleton ruin of a once great pueblo of the Tiguex Indians, who, in 1540, gave a friendly welcome to Coronado and his entourage. In a matter of minutes, seconds really, we could see on our right the living pueblos of Santa Ana and Tsia, sun baked on the adobe banks of the Jemez River near its junction with the Rio Grande. As we crossed a low, hilly divide at the southern tip of the Jemez Range, a vast expanse of semidesert came into view, broken here and there by piñon-covered buttes, while stark forms of volcanic cones rose above the terrain. To the north of us lay Old Navaholand, dimly seen on the horizon, extending to the border of New Mexico and Colorado and a little beyond.

As we flew over this arid land, leaving the Jemez Mountains behind us, Tsoodził, Navaho Sacred Mountain of the South, rose in tiered mesas to its eleven-thousand-foot snow-tipped summit. We circled several times seeking the proper foreground for this picture, finding such different country from the empty areas of the San Luis Valley. Thick clusters of cedar and piñon trees, broken by parklike openings and rugged prominences, built up to the mountain peak. We saw isolated hogans, sometimes three or four in a group representing a family unit, with sheep corrals and, nearby, flocks grazing. There was an occasional horseman, a car, a truck or two—so few signs of life in

[3] Navaho can be spelled two ways: the phonetic spelling with an *h*, which assures correct pronunciation, or the Spanish spelling with a *j*. The latter has been adopted by the United States government, and a few years ago the Navaho Tribal Council officially adopted the *j*-spelling, in spite of years of using the *h*. Many authors, Dr. Washington Matthews, Father Berard Haile, and Dr. Clyde Kluckhohn, among others, have long used the *h*-spelling. To assure correct pronunciation, the *h*-spelling is used in this book, with the exception of certain official names and titles.

*Tsoodził (Mount Taylor), Sacred Mountain of the South.*

this big empty-looking land. It seemed hard to believe that more than 104,000 Navaho People live on this reservation.

Turning to a northwesterly direction we were soon over land free of timber but covered with desert grass and low shrubs. We crossed Chaco Canyon, looking down on the extensive ruin of Pueblo Bonito and other ancient sites of this once populous region. The Navaho have stories about these ruins and their long forgotten prehistoric inhabitants—the Kiis'aanii, ancestors of the Pueblo People. We crossed the Escavada Wash, a wide, dry river bed, capable of carrying a raging torrent following a summer thunderstorm. Soon we could see the green valley of the San Juan River, imagining how the Navaho must have followed it as the more adventurous among them sought new homesites.

History tells us of the many conflicts between the Navaho and the Pueblo Indians and Spanish settlers. It was Coronado who first brought both sheep and horses to this country, and later, following the Spanish colonization, the Navaho, filled with envy, stole or traded for the animals they coveted. Horses gave them a new and better mode of travel and it was not long until they became stockmen. Horses also gave them incentive to hunt new pastures and remote canyons in which to hide their stolen booty, as well as giving them new and mobile means for war upon enemy Indians and raids upon the Pueblos and the Spanish settlers.

We crossed the fertile valley of the San Juan, circling for a landing at Farmington to refuel the plane and to have a short rest. As we turned, Tsoodził, still though distantly visible, lifted its snowy summit into the turquoise sky—the one high landmark—Tsoodził, Navaho Sacred Mountain of the South.

After a short rest and a second breakfast, we continued our journey, following the San Juan River toward the Four Corners, that unique spot where the states of Arizona and Utah meet Colorado and New Mexico. Below us were many farms, for this is the most cultivated part of the reservation. Green fields of alfalfa and ripening fields of corn and oats filled the pale landscape with rich color. After completion of the new Navajo Reservoir, and as its stored water becomes available for irrigation, the Navaho will expand this region to include many thousands of acres of new arable land, acres now bordering the narrow productive strip of the river's valley.

Shiprock, largest of the volcanic cores of the Southwest, rose more than 1,800 feet out of the desert sea, its two great flanking dykes bringing to mind the Navaho legend of an eagle with outspread wings. Beyond was the Red Rock area I knew so well, and I could trace the merging of the dun-colored landscape into opalescent red as we neared the Lukachukai Mountains, that small group which forms the northern boundary of the Chuska Range. This 9,500-foot range runs north and south, bisecting the reservation. It is densely covered with pine and fir, spruce and aspen, yielding a large timber reserve for the Navaho People.

To the south of us, as we crossed the Lukachukais, we could see the whole Chuska Mountain Range sloping into the Defiance Plateau, the timber changing to piñon and cedar as the elevation dropped. Beneath us were huge red sandstone promontories jutting out into the sage-covered foothills, like giant ocean piers.

Ahead of us, sun drenched and glowing red, we could see Monument Valley as the timbered plateau dropped beneath us to meet the western desert. The beauty of the monoliths was startling from the air, so different from the ground aspect, where one looks up at them into a contrasting blue sky. After circling the valley, we continued our western direction and in the span of a quarter of an hour were over the southern end of another timbered plateau which extends south from Utah into Arizona. Tsegi Canyon emerged beneath us, and following a tributary we saw suddenly the cliff dwelling of Beta-ta-kin, one of the most beautiful of all the thirteenth-century ruins of the Southwest. The gracefully arched cave, with its sheer clefts of rock at one end, protects the buildings from storm and wind. Rich green foliage nestles close to the spring which these early inhabitants were fortunate enough to have at their doorsteps. So completely do the buildings blend into the rose-colored rock of the high cave, that the shadowed rectangular doorways are all that make the cliff dwelling visible. This ruin, and others not far away, now comprise the Navajo National Monument.

Cutting across the western edge of Black Mountain, we turned southward over an expanse of yellow sand, as yet another desert extended to the Grand Canyon, the western boundary of the reservation. A short flying time brought us opposite Doko'oosłíid, and we saw the Little Colorado River marking a diagonal course in our foreground as it contributes its small share of water to its mighty brother, the Colorado.

*Dokoʼoosłííd (San Francisco Peaks), Sacred Mountain of the West.*

Once more we saw a high landmark—Doko'oosłííd, Navaho Sacred Mountain of the West.

We turned southeast, leaving the western boundary behind us, and as we crossed Hopiland, that island reservation surrounded by the Navaho, we looked down on the rocky mesa towns of this sturdy Pueblo group. We landed at Winslow, Arizona, for a midday meal and a needed rest.

Later in the afternoon we took off once more, heading home to Santa Fe, more than three hundred miles away. During the morning we had flown at a low elevation, about one thousand feet or less, giving me a closer and more detailed vision of the land. Now, with bumpy air rising from the warm ground, we climbed to about three thousand feet, and to my amazement we could see all the country we had crossed on the morning's flight. We flew over the Painted Desert, saw the Petrified Forest, and, far to the south, the long valley traversed by Coronado as he came from Mexico seeking the Seven Cities of Cibola, bringing with him many horses and thousands of sheep.

To the north we could see the piñon-covered mesas of the Defiance Plateau, whose formation is that of a wide bowl, gathering a great amount of natural moisture which funnels down into the sheer Canyon de Chelly and Canyon del Muerto, spilling eventually into the Chinle Wash. This is a dry, sandy stream bed on the surface for most of the year, though there is a continual underground flow. The wash slopes gently to the north for a hundred miles, emptying finally into the San Juan River at the northern boundary of the reservation. The Navaho penetrated into the region of the Canyons in the beginning of the eighteenth century, possibly earlier, when, according to some archaeologists, they may have found Hopi Indians farming in the Canyons and either drove them out or absorbed them into the tribe. It was from the north rim of Canyon del Muerto that a small company of Spanish soldiers, sent out from Santa Fe to retaliate against Navaho raiders, attacked a cave in the Canyon wall, killing most of the inhabitants. This was in 1804, the time of the Louisiana Purchase, when New Mexico and Arizona were under the rule of Spain, and Thomas Jefferson was wondering about this western land. From time to time the Spanish sent many expeditions against the Navaho, trying to stop the depredations of Spanish towns and Pueblo villages along the Rio Grande. They bargained and they bribed, but like the ebb and flow of ocean tide the raids continued, though there were intervals of peaceful pursuits and welcomed exchange of goods.

Following Mexican independence in 1821, the government in Santa Fe, then directed from Mexico City, was struggling weakly to assert itself. Navaho raids increased in number and in strength. Twenty-five years later, after our war with Mexico, both Navaho and Apache depredations were at their height. The Southwest now became part of the United States, and new expeditions left Santa Fe for Navaholand. The Navaho had no comprehension of such political and governmental changes. This was all a very wild, rough country then, the distances were very great for horse or foot travel, and water sources were far apart. In 1851 the United States Army established Fort Defiance as a first base of operations. As we now approached the Arizona-New Mexico line, I could see the large grove of trees, some of them planted long ago and now obscuring the Fort from the air, submerging it in a pool of shade. Close by, amid a cluster of wind-worn sandstone, was Window Rock, the present seat of Navaho government.

As I watched the passing landscape, the procession of Navaho historic events filled my mind, and I thought of all that had happened to these people since they had come under the rule of Washington, 119 years ago. The early efforts of such a small segment of the American Army had proved fruitless in the attempt to quell the Navaho raids, for in this rugged country the soldiers were no match for the Navaho, so skilled in guerrilla warfare. In 1863 the Army commissioned the famous scout, Colonel Christopher (Kit) Carson, to bring the Navaho to terms. Through a scorched-earth policy, he destroyed crops, killed or captured livestock, and finally rounded up most of the starving people.

Then the commanding general decided to move the Navaho to a new environment—to Fort Sumner, more than three hundred miles away in eastern New Mexico on the Pecos River—and the captured Navaho were forced to march to Bosque Redondo, as they called it. It was the first time they had ever been conquered; they were being sent into exile. The year 1864 became a tragic milestone in Navaho history.

Our plane approached Gallup, New Mexico, and as I looked north across the reservation I could see Shiprock standing above the desert, more shiplike than ever

*Monument Valley.*

*Dibéntsaa (Mount Hesperus), Sacred Mountain of the North.*

from this height and distance. And beyond, rising above the great promontories and canyons of Mesa Verde, glistening on the far horizon, were the snowy summits of Dibéntsaa, Navaho Sacred Mountain of the North.

For many miles east of Gallup, as we continued our journey, we flew directly over the route of the exile march, the Long Walk, as the Navaho call it. Looking down, one could visualize the straggling line of slowly moving, destitute people. It was in early March of 1864 that the Long Walk began. The People were moved in groups, some 2,400 in the first, others following during the spring, until a total of some 8,500 Navaho had made the long march. Only the very old and the very young were permitted to ride in the few wagons the People still possessed. They had nothing left, only a few horses, some sheep, and some goats—that was all.

Those four years of exile were tragic years indeed. Lack of understanding, lack of supplies, and lack of communication caused much hardship and suffering. The exile began near the close of the Civil War. The government in Washington had little thought for one small group of captured Indians so far away. The wonder is that Congress appropriated $100,000 for Navaho rehabilitation. The money was entrusted to two individuals who were to proceed to Independence, Missouri, there to purchase the necessary supplies. These were the days of the Santa Fe Trail, when long, heavily laden wagon trains labored across nine hundred miles of prairie. Of the original appropriation, less than a third ever reached its destination.

Yet the Navaho were willing enough to do what they could to better their condition. They learned to make adobe bricks; some became blacksmiths; they did their best to farm under the most adverse conditions of drought, wind, insect infestations, and illness among themselves. An epidemic of smallpox struck and many died, reducing their number to a little over 6,000; many were ill from undernourishment; all were desperately homesick. Finally, on hearing of a plan to move them to Oklahoma, several Navaho leaders agreed to go to Washington to plead for permission to return to their own land.

One can imagine the revelation such a trip must have been to these men: the long horseback ride to Independence, the first sight of a railroad train, and the long trip to Washington; the realization for the first time of the great size of the United States; the arrival in the capital city and a meeting with President Andrew Johnson. Shortly after the Navaho returned to Fort Sumner, General Sherman was sent to draw up a treaty in which the Navaho promised to stop their raids, a promise quite faithfully kept with but a few minor exceptions. In return, the government of the United States promised to give them a new start by supplying tools, seed, and three sheep per family; also one teacher for every thirty children. After one hundred years this last part of the treaty is only now being fulfilled.

So the humbled Navaho, in the fall of 1868, returned to their mesas and canyons, their deserts and mountains, to begin life anew. But more hardships were yet to be endured, for in spite of efforts by Major Dodd, the first civil agent, the promised supplies and sheep did not arrive. That first winter was grim indeed. The Navaho ate what they could find on the land—piñon nuts, roots, other small edible plants, and some game. The promised sheep did not arrive until the fall of 1869. Then the People felt a surge of hope as they began to till new fields, to start new flocks, to build new hogans, and to live the free life which was the very essence of their being.

While the memory of all this history flashed through my mind, we were flying rapidly home to Santa Fe, as the long shadows of late afternoon reached across the mountains. It seemed incredible that in the course of a few hours, I could have seen so closely and so clearly practically the entire 25,000 square miles of Navaho domain, and looked down on areas where so much history had taken place. It gave me new insight and understanding of the Navaho and their land. It was a memorable day.

# THE DINEH

SPACE-SKY-DISTANCE UNLIMITED; canyons-deserts-rocks majestic in their contour and hugeness; color-landforms beautiful beyond belief—these are the elements of this magnificent land. Moving about in loneliness, though never lonely, in dignity and happiness, with song in their hearts and on their lips, in harmony with the great forces of nature, are the Dinéh—People of the Earth.

Two salient qualities of these people are dignity and happiness. Both spring from their vital traditional faith, faith in nature, faith in themselves as a part of nature, faith in their place in the universe, deep-rooted faith born of their Oriental origin, moulded and strengthened by the land in which they live. There is fine quality in the Navaho People, evident in their quiet direct manner, their action, their manual dexterity and skill. They bring to their everyday living dignity, vitality, realism, and acceptance of things as they are. Conforming to the pattern of their tradition, they are nonetheless individualists. They have character, they have the ordinary run of human weaknesses, they have humor and a sense of fun, they have their own code of honor. They are tenacious. They are practical to a high degree; they are poetical. They are capable of long hours of work, and they are capable equally of inactivity. There are many good Navaho People and some bad, dependable and some undependable, strong and some weak. Their powers of observation are photographic. They are immeasurably adaptable. They can be shrewd, they can be inscrutable, they are highly intuitive. Among themselves they are a gentle people. Through all runs a vein of kindliness, inherent good manners, and a special quality for which it is difficult to find the right word. Perhaps

*Lilly Benally.*

integrated personality is the attribute, for there is a "oneness" about these people. Simply and quietly they abide by their tradition.

All this is what they have been and what many still are today. But as they acquire more of our way of life, as they participate in our education (and many are doing so at remarkable speed), will they retain the fine qualities of their inheritance? They are now taking from our civilization what they wish of it and using it as a part of their own. Some are finding themselves against a wall of frustration and have not yet found a way around it. Barred at first by language, many have now received a high degree of our education and are intelligent, capable people, judged by the highest standards. The hope of their future lies in their unique adaptability and their desire and quickness to learn. It is my belief that the Navaho People as a whole will retain their place in our American Democracy and that many will carry forward that place with distinction.

But generalities are not enough; one must know the individuals. My first acquaintances were made when I visited Elizabeth Forster not long after she assumed her duties as a field nurse. She was stationed at Red Rock, Arizona, just over the line from New Mexico, some thirty miles west of the community of Shiprock. Here she had an apartment in an abandoned missionary hospital, with a clinic room in the basement where she kept the tools of her trade. Here the doctor from the government hospital in Shiprock came weekly to see patients who had been assembled by the nurse for his visit. The usual run of minor ailments, sore throats, slight injuries, the ever present impetigo among small children, various dietary ailments, and often illnesses of a more serious nature, were examined. Treatments were prescribed for the nurse to administer, necessitating visits to hogans within the radius of her field work. It was my good fortune to accompany Betsy on some of her rounds, giving me an opportunity to observe her many patients under the conditions of their everyday lives.

Often we went to the trading post nearby, where we met many more Navaho People, and soon I learned how to overcome their natural shyness or antipathy to photographs. In those days of the 1930's I was using a large view camera and I was able to interest the people in both the instrument and the results, for they always wanted copies of the pictures I made. It was not long until the people of the Red Rock area were used to seeing me around and I was accepted as the nurse's friend. Some of these early pictures are in this book—the frontispiece, the first eight or ten portraits, the summer hogan, and others.

Gradually, I was learning the customs of the Navaho and some of the simple things one must or must not do, such as always shaking hands, but it is unfriendly not to take off one's glove; when offering a cigarette, one must never point it at a person, but must hold it upright, or sideways. If one sees a fox, he must either turn around and go back to where he came from or wait until four other creatures, either animals or birds, pass him going in the same direction as the fox. There are good omens as well as bad, and the white man is usually excused for not knowing these customs, but better relationships may be had if the stranger takes the trouble to learn Navaho ways. Good manners and simple courtesy are very much a part of Navaho life, and there is always a right way and a wrong way to do everything. This is why Navaho People deliberate before every act, before every spoken word. This patient deliberation is often misjudged by non-Indian people. The Navaho is not slow, he is taking time in deciding what is the right thing to do or say. Once this decision is reached it is inconsistent for a Navaho to change his mind.

When Betsy was at Red Rock she had an interpreter, as there were many in her region who spoke no English. This young man, Timothy Kellywood by name, lived in a small hogan near the trading post with his wife and two small boys. Timothy drove Betsy's car for her, translated both questions and answers, and soon considered himself her assistant. Betsy's human understanding of the People and their needs quickly won her many friends, and her obvious interest in their lives and beliefs was appreciated greatly. That she did not oppose the medicine men came as a surprise to many and it was not long until one medicine man of the region occasionally came to her for help. He indicated his acceptance of her by placing his two forefingers together, to show that they would work side by side.

Timothy constantly brought to Betsy all the news of the area, and one of the great surprises to both of us was how rapidly news could travel. I recall one day

*Timothy Kellywood and his family.*

when we were driving along a little-used road and Timothy said suddenly, "I think Mr. Jones has been to Red Rock today." When I asked how he knew, he answered, "I see the track of his left rear tire." Timothy soon became my friend, also, and would say, "I know where there is a silversmith you would like to make a picture of." So off we would go to find someone I did indeed want to photograph. Timothy's judgment was unerring and I seldom failed to follow his lead.

One trip of Betsy's, which I recall, was to a distant mesa where a teenage boy was very ill. She and Timothy had to climb some distance to the hogan, leaving the car at the foot of the mesa. After examining the boy, taking his temperature, and hearing what his parents had to tell her, she felt sure that he had a ruptured appendix. She persuaded the boy, and his parents, to let her take him to the hospital at once. Placing him carefully on a blanket which she used in lieu of a stretcher, she directed four men, each holding a corner of the blanket, to carry the boy down to the car. Then with very careful driving she took him more than thirty miles to the hospital. The doctor found that it was indeed a ruptured appendix and operated immediately. Through Betsy's good judgment and skill this boy's life was saved.

At the time of another of my periodic visits, Betsy had a patient, a small child who had fallen into the hot coals of the open fire in the center of her mother's hogan. The burns on her little hands were bad, and Betsy went daily to dress them. The day I accompanied her I found the lovely mother seated at her loom on the far side of the hogan. As there was the usual blanket over the door, the only light within was from the smoke hole in the center of the roof. The beautiful overhead light accented the Oriental quality of this woman as she sat patiently while Betsy attended to the child's hands and I attempted to capture the picture I saw.

Not long after Betsy's arrival at Red Rock, there was a "sing" going on some little distance away. This Betsy learned was a curing ceremony for a sick Navaho. One of the singers came to her clinic room asking for cough medicine. His name—incredibly—was Killed-a-White-Man. He came to Betsy several times during the ceremony. She ran out of cough medicine and, when next in Shiprock, asked the doctor for more, but he told her she must use it more sparingly. The next time Killed-a-White-Man came for cough medicine she told him, through Timothy, that she was sorry but she didn't have any more. He left without a word. The next time he came she still didn't have any. He didn't like not getting his medicine, but again left without comment. The third time he came he said to Timothy, "You ask her why she doesn't have the things a nurse is supposed to have?" Betsy got behind a chair, and, pretending to tremble and shake, said to Timothy, "Ask him if he ever killed a white woman?" This question sent the old man into a peal of laughter and from then on he was one of Betsy's good friends. She found out later that he really had killed a white man long ago. The Navaho had been out hunting and

*The quiet overhead light in a hogan.*

*Portrait of a young boy.*

*Costume of the 1930's.*

*Once as Betsy and I left a hogan where she had been on a nursing visit, we encountered this woman carrying her small son and two lambs. Twenty-five years later we found the woman again, and while we were talking to her, her husband rode up with a small boy in the saddle in front of him. This baby turned out to be the son of the boy held by his mother in the earlier picture.*

had failed to find any game. He did find a white prospector in camp cooking his supper, of which he had plenty but which he refused to share. The white man also had some wine which he refused to offer. At that time Killed-a-White-Man earned his name.

One winter when I was at Red Rock it was necessary for Betsy, Timothy, and me to take an ill old man to the hospital. The snow was deep and it was very cold. It took us three hours to reach Shiprock. As we were preparing to return, a Red Rock boy appeared, having followed us in. Just after we had left Red Rock word had come that Hosteen Nez's wife had been in labor for five days and needed help. Betsy and the doctor left at once, Timothy and I followed in her car. About five miles before reaching Red Rock the doctor left the main road to drive several more miles to the Nez hogan. The snow drifts were very deep and Betsy and the doctor repeatedly had to dig themselves out. When they finally arrived it was after dark. They found the woman as described, surrounded by an assembly of neighbors who hoped to help. There was no light but that of the fire in the center of the hogan. After dismissing the onlookers, nurse and doctor improvised an operating table out of two orange crates, then extinguished the fire so that ether could be safely used. Having only a two-battery flash light for illumination, the doctor's interpreter had to direct the light first to the nurse, administering the ether, and then to the doctor, who by use of instruments delivered a live baby. The crisis was over—that is, except for more struggles to get home through the snow.

As individuals became better known to Betsy, and through her to me, their respective characters stood out. There was a little old woman whose only name was The Ute Woman, who used to come to breakfast every Sunday morning. She really was a Ute; she had been stolen by a Navaho family in her infancy and had grown up a Navaho, knowing nothing of the Ute people.

Every Navaho has a ceremonial name seldom if ever known except to his family. In addition to this name, he will have one known to the Navaho People. Navaho custom does not permit the direct addressing of a person; he is spoken of indirectly as "my sister's son," or "my nephew's wife." Then each Navaho will have a nickname, often descriptive, by which he is called as a child. When he goes to school he will be given another name, by which he is generally known. Often these names are selected from among well-known white people. For instance, a former Indian commissioner has two namesakes that I know of. But the descriptive nicknames always fascinated us. There was Hardbelly, Sorehand, Bushyhead, Calicopants, and many more. One day we realized how many descriptive names there are among our own people, such as Whitehead, Shoemaker, Wheelwright, Younghunter, Longstreet, and Stonebreaker, to name a few.

Betsy has a wonderful capacity for joking with a perfectly straight face. The Navaho sensed this and delighted in it. There was a Navaho named John Billy, whom she had met when she first went to Red Rock to see what the nursing position there would involve. She did not see him again for more than a year. One day he came to her clinic and she was dismayed to find he had a bad exopthalmic goiter condition. He was willing to go to the hospital where he was operated on under a local anesthetic. In a very short time he was sent back to Red Rock, arriving in the early evening. Betsy fixed him up for the night in her clinic room. Several Navaho in the immediate vicinity came to see him, and all evening Betsy could hear voices from the basement as John Billy told about his operation. Because it was impossible to drive him home through the deep snow, Betsy urged him to borrow a horse to ride the eighteen miles to his hogan. She explained that he must not overexert himself and that she hoped he would take two days, stopping at some friend's hogan on the way. In the morning when she called him for some breakfast he had already gone, and, as she later found out, he walked the whole distance to his home through the snow in one day.

Off and on all winter she heard tales that John Billy was sick, but he did not come in, nor could she reach him; however, as soon as it was possible to get the car through she did go to his hogan. Thinking that he should see the doctor for a check up, she urged him to come with her to the hospital. But he said, "No." Finally after much conversation and with a straight face, Betsy said, "John Billy, I am going to take you to the doctor, even if I have to rope you." His wife, who spoke no English, asked him what the nurse said. There were some whispered words, then he said, "All right, I go." "When?" asked the nurse. "Now," an-

*Elizabeth Forster in Hardbelly's hogan in 1932.*

swered John Billy. Husband and wife went into the hogan, emerging in a few minutes as Mrs. John Billy led her husband by a rope, which she handed to Betsy with great merriment. Later, he used to come to Betsy's apartment, asking her to write some letters for him, which she, of course, was pleased to do. One day Timothy said, "Miss Forster, why do you write John Billy's letters? Don't you know he is a Carlisle graduate?" Betsy decided that John Billy had had the last laugh.

One day we drove out to Hardbelly's hogan where the old man was suffering from a heart condition. The doctor having prescribed digitalis, Betsy was to instruct the old man's elder wife (he had three) how to measure the proper dose. As we entered the hogan we found Hardbelly lying on his pallet, his wife and family sitting about him. Betsy proceeded with her mission while I wondered if I dared ask to make a picture. To my surprise they seemed pleased that I wanted to, which was one more evidence of their confidence in their nurse.

Thirty-three years later we found ourselves again

in this vicinity. We came to a group of hogans, and saw, sitting in a summer shelter nearby, three older women. After shaking hands and finding that no one spoke English, I returned to the car to get Betsy, feeling sure that she would find someone she had known long ago. No one recognized her, nor she any of them, so by way of conversation I produced my portfolio. When we came to the picture made in Hardbelly's hogan in 1932, excitement spread amid a rapid flow of Navaho. I pointed to the nurse in the picture, then to Betsy standing beside me, but the oldest of the three kept shaking her head. Just then a teenage boy came to see what was happening. "My grandmother says this is not the nurse, she had dark hair." Betsy leaned over, taking a lock of the old lady's hair, and said, "Tell your grandmother she did too." Recognition broke through; the old woman stood up, put her head on Betsy's shoulder and her arms around her, and wept. After a few minutes Mrs. Hardbelly raised her head, shook herself, straightened her shoulders, and returned to the present. Later, we arranged to come back in two days, when their clothes would be freshly washed and they would all be ready for more pictures, for these three women were the widows of old Hardbelly. Plural marriages were common many years ago, and frequently one or more sisters married the man of the family. The Indian Service finally forbade plural marriages, which are supposed to be nonexistent today.

One tragedy that stands out in Betsy's memory occurred during the bitter winter of 1932 when the snow lay a foot or more deep over the land. In the middle of the night Betsy was awakened by a pounding on her door. Outside stood a Navaho man breathing heavily and dripping with sweat. His three-month-old baby was very sick; he had run more than three miles through the snow for help. After questioning him carefully, Betsy sent him to wake Timothy to get the car ready, while she prepared for expected emergency. Reaching the hogan after wallowing through the snow in the cold darkness, she found the baby very ill with pneumonia. She learned that in spite of the medicine man's ritual the baby had gotten worse.

Knowing that the only possible chance to save the baby was getting it to the hospital thirty miles away, she persuaded the parents to bring the baby, still in its cradleboard. They should go at once. Although the interior of the car was warmed by the heater, the tires made the crisp, squeaky crunch that means extreme cold as they cut through the icy snow. All were silent except for the whimpering of the sick infant. Somewhere along the way that sound ceased and Betsy feared the worst. They all went into the hospital to find the doctor, but it was too late. After the doctor's examination, the parents decided to leave the little body at the hospital where the authorities would see to its burial in the cemetery nearby. As they were leaving the building, a very hard-boiled nurse scolded the baby's mother, telling her it was her fault for not bringing the baby to the hospital earlier.

On the way home to Red Rock, out in the windswept flat beyond Shiprock, the father asked Timothy to stop the car. The mother and father got out carrying the empty cradleboard. Walking a short distance from the road, they cleared away the snow and with bowed heads placed the cradleboard on the ground, covering it with fresh snow. It would never be used again, so the bereaved parents gave it to the elements. When they returned to the car, Betsy tried to comfort them. The medicine man had done what he could, but for this kind of illness, the white doctor had newer medicine.

Such thoughtless, unsympathetic remarks as those given by the hospital nurse have been one reason many Navaho have hesitated or refused government help for so long a time. Looking back on that tragic night after a span of thirty years, we can understand the conflict of thought in the minds of those parents. All their lifelong belief made them rely on the medicine man, who for many ailments was competent indeed, but respiratory infection was something the Navaho little understood. Perhaps one of the greatest changes on the reservation in the past thirty years is the quality of the white personnel working with the Navaho. Today these doctors and nurses are better equipped with social and psychological understanding to win rather than force—to teach rather than admonish. Doctors of today are aware of the abilities of the medicine men and are seeking their co-operation in many ways, while teaching them to understand the kind of help the white doctor can give.

*The women . . .*

*. . . as we found them in 1955.*

*Navaho twins.*

*Georgie Garcia.*

*Tom Navaho.*

*May Adson.*

*An old Navaho woman.*

*A portrait at Navaho Mountain.*

*The letter.*

*Ason Kinlichine.*

*A typical Navaho posture.*

*Molian of Red Rock.*

*Old Lady Grey Salt.*

*Irene Yazzie.*

*Luke Yazzie.*

*Portrait of Sam Yazzie.*

*Ned Hatathli's daughter and friend.*

*A young Navaho mother.*

*Bah Francis.*

*The summer shelter in the Cove (1934).*

*The Ute Woman.*

A most amusing incident that happened several years ago was told to me by a friend who witnessed the climax. A man and his wife from New Jersey were on their first trip to the West. They had been to the Grand Canyon and were returning across the Navaho Reservation. Never having experienced anything like the lonesomeness of the great open spaces of the Southwest, they were quite overwhelmed by it. Also they were somewhat afraid of the strange people who spoke a "foreign" language whom they had seen at one trading post where they stopped to buy gasoline and to ask for directions. After leaving Kayenta, in northern Arizona, they were heading south toward Chinle, when their car broke down. They seemed to be in the middle of nowhere. The man, deciding that he must walk ahead for help, left his wife in the car.

A short while later an elderly Navaho on horseback, having seen the stalled car, rode up, dismounted, and, leaning his arms on the open door of the car, politely asked the lady (in Navaho, of course) if he could be of any help. The wife, terrified by the sudden appearance of the strange man and the stranger words, opened the door and quickly walked away. The old man, watching her, realized that he had scared her, and called to tell her that he only wanted to help. At the sound of his voice again, the woman began to run. The Navaho decided that he couldn't let her go out into the region where she could get lost, or fall and hurt herself, or possibly stir up a rattlesnake, so he jumped on his horse and started after her. When the woman saw this she was more terrified than ever, and she ran as hard as she was able. Finally, the Navaho took the rope from his saddle and neatly lassoed the frightened woman, again telling her that he wouldn't hurt her, that he only wanted to help. Turning, he led her back to the road and headed in the direction her husband had taken. On the other side of a low mesa, out of sight from the car, was a trading post only four or five miles away. Inside the post was the usual colorful gathering of Navaho People, some sitting on the benches along the wall, some making purchases at the counter, a group of gossiping women with babies in cradleboards, a group of men standing in the center of the room conversing. A little apart stood several white men, among them the bearer of this tale who was talking to the woman's husband. The old Navaho man entered the post leading the white woman by his rope, to the surprise of all and the great merriment of several. He asked the trader which white man was the woman's husband, whereupon he handed the rope to the astonished man, asking the trader to tell him that by the time they got there "she was leading pretty good!"

In the fall of 1934 we made our first visit to the Red Rock area following Betsy's departure. From several old Navaho friends whom we met between Shiprock and Red Rock, we were told that The Ute Woman had died. Betsy refused to believe this rumor. At Red Rock we found an old friend, Francis Nakai, who told us that The Ute Woman had been very ill but was better and was now living over beyond the Cove. He offered to go with us to find her. After a fifteen-mile drive over practically no road at all, we reached the edge of a wash, a deep arroyo, where we left the car and proceeded on foot. As we walked down a trail into the wash, we saw a diminutive figure hurrying toward us. She had recognized our old car and when we met, her arms went around Betsy's neck and she cried and cried. We walked back with her to an unbelievably frugal shelter where she was living alone with her cat. In an outpouring of Navaho words, she told Betsy all that had happened to her since her friend had gone away. She had had medicine men help her and in payment for their services had sacrificed her every possession.

A few hundred yards away from The Ute Woman's home was a beautiful summer shelter belonging to Willie Lee and his family, who were looking after the old woman whenever she needed help. As we passed the Red Rock Trading Post on our way back, we left an order with the trader to send out some coffee, sugar, and flour at the first opportunity. We continued our vacation trip to the Grand Canyon, then decided to return to see The Ute Woman once more on our way home to Colorado. We found her at the Willie Lee shelter, where we were profusely thanked for the food we had sent, as they graciously presented each of us with a gift, a beaded belt and a small blanket. We stayed an hour or more enjoying the beauty of this scene before us of Navaho summer life and the warm welcome of our friends.

These are but a few of the many daily experiences of one nurse as she demonstrated the need for field nursing service among the Navaho People. Since 1934 the United States Public Health Service has increased such service many times; and in the past fifteen years Annie Wauneka, member of the Tribal Council, who heads the Navaho health and education program, has accomplished remarkable progress in developing medical and nursing service for her people.

The organization sponsoring Betsy's work was forced to discontinue her service due to lack of funds during the Depression. She left Red Rock late in 1933 to assume a new public health position in Colorado. Twice during the next eight years we returned to the Red Rock area, always receiving a warm welcome from many friends. These were years of work for each of us far from the reservation. Then came the war years, and our activities and thoughts were even farther from Navaholand. Near the end of the war, Betsy was stricken with a near-fatal illness, polio-encephalitis, incapacitating her from further nursing service. In 1945 I moved to Santa Fe as headquarters for other work in which I was engaged. The following year my friend joined me, and it was not long until the strong pull of memories took us back among the Navaho People. As I realized the speed with which changes were coming to the reservation, the possibility of this book began to formulate, though work on it has of necessity been intermittent. This undertaking has been close to our hearts, for both Betsy and I feel an enduring friendship, understanding, and admiration for the Navaho People.

# PART II

# THE WAY OF THE PEOPLE

# HABITATION

NAVAHO HOMES, OR HOGANS, are scattered far and wide over the reservation, in order to obtain adequate pasturage for the sheep. Each family has grazing rights, and though there is no individual ownership of land as we know it, the individual's rights are usually respected. Seldom does one encroach on another's pasture; boundaries are indicated only by a small pile of stones, and boundary lines follow the contour of the land, for there are no stock fences. The same rights prevail for summer pasture in mountain areas where sheep are moved to higher elevations for fresh grass.

The hogan is a most practical building for life in this desert country. It heats with a minimum amount of fuel, it is cool in summer, and, having no windows, it is a retreat from the strong winds of early spring. There is a quiet peace within the hogan, for the only light is from above, through the smoke hole in the roof. The form of the hogan stems from the Creation Story, for it was the Holy People who built the first one, thus setting the pattern and the customs. Round, or nearly round in shape, and with a dome-like roof, the hogan always faces East, to the rising sun and the new day. When a new hogan is built, pieces of turquoise or shell are placed beneath the doorposts. When it is completed, the hogan is blessed by a medicine man if one is near, or by the head of the family. Corn pollen, symbol of fertility, is sprinkled on the logs or stone while the chanter invokes peace and a happy life.

Depending on the environment, hogans are built of a variety of materials. Where logs are available, there are two or three general types: the old forked-stick hogan (nearly extinct); hogans built of upright logs topped with cribbed horizontal logs to build dome-shaped roofs; and hogans with logs laid horizontally

*Sunrise over the desert.*

*A hexagonal hogan near Red Rock.*

*An upright log and mud plaster hogan in the Checkerboard Area.*

in hexagonal or octagonal form, all being chinked with adobe mud or clay. In areas where timber is scarce, hogans are built of stone, again, either round or hexagonal with always the domed roof. A special form of roof construction is used, as may be seen in the interior pictures. In recent times, one finds occasionally that windows have been cut into walls.

In a barren area I found a round stone hogan. The woman was bringing the sheep home to a nearby corral for the night. The building seems small in the broad, majestic landscape, yet the interior of the same hogan gives a suggestion of its height and roominess, though the picture contains less than a quarter of the whole.

On entering a hogan, one must move from left to right, clockwise, circling the fire in the center of the room. On formal occasions the women sit on the north side of the hogan, the cooking side, and the men on the south, while the head of the family and any guests sit on the west, facing the entrance. In early times a shallow fire pit was dug in the earth floor. The pits still are dug, though in recent times many Navaho are using tin or iron stoves, sometimes small metal barrels, with stove pipes extending out of the roof holes. To the right of the entrance, which may have a wooden door or the old-time blanket covering, simple shelves made from empty orange crates or boxes obtained from nearby trading posts will hold dishes and food staples. On the west side of the hogan sheepskins, which serve as beds at night, will have been rolled up and stacked away. Hanging from pegs or nails along the sides will be extra clothing, blankets, and other items of daily use. In other places along the sides of the hogan are boxes, suitcases, or even small trunks, in which other possessions are stored. There is a place for everything and there is usually order. Following the ancient pattern to which all individuals subscribe, this true sense of order permeates Navaho life.

Where Navaho people have moved to nearby towns and are living in regular houses, I have seen disorder and a slovenly way of living. The reason seems twofold, poverty and the example of white people of low caliber, for few Navaho have had much contact with cultured Anglo homes. I recall an episode in 1932, when Betsy and I took Mrs. Francis Nakai and Timothy to Santa Fe to see the wonderful collection of Navaho blankets in the Indian Arts Fund Collection. Following this experience we stopped to say "hello" to friends of ours who lived in one of the loveliest of Southwestern homes. We were all invited to return that evening for dinner, when there was to be a birthday party for the son of the house. Mrs. Francis' acceptance of that evening was something I shall always remember. She had never been away from Red Rock, and her only contact with any white man's home had been the very simple apartment Betsy had in the old hospital building, where for the first time Mrs. Francis sat at a table to eat. At our friends' house that evening, we sat down to a formal dinner for twelve people at a table exquisitely set with shining silver, sparkling glass, lighted candles, and all the trimmings for a birthday party. Mrs. Francis quietly watched what others did, and, with the utmost dignity, followed suit as though she were accustomed to such elaborateness. During the evening Timothy repeated to me over and over, "Oh, I never saw such a beautiful house!" His eyes were shining. As we took our departure he spoke to our hostess, saying, "My relative thanks you very much for everything and she wishes that she understood English so she could have known all that has been talked about." As we returned to our motel, I wondered if I could have conducted myself with such perfect poise and dignity if I had found myself in completely foreign surroundings with such different customs, and listening to a language I did not understand. At the present time, however, during this transition period from the old life to the new, Navaho people are buying second-hand beds, tables, and chairs, and the old sense of order is disappearing.

Near the winter hogan there is always a summer shelter, for the Navaho live chiefly out-of-doors during the summer months. Built of upright poles, the shelter has a roof of fresh green boughs from cottonwood trees, or cedar or juniper. In areas where sheep are taken to the mountains for summer pasture, the winter hogan will be closed. As the Navaho live with a minimum of possessions, they have little to move for life during the summer months. Cooking utensils, some extra clothing, wool for weaving, a few basic food suppiles, such as salt, sugar, coffee, and flour, are all that are needed. The women set up their looms under the shelter, the children watch the flocks, and the men haul water and wood and tend the small farms.

Water in most areas must be brought from wells or

*A round stone hogan near Little Shiprock.*

*Interior of Harriet Cadman's hogan.*

DUZ

from the few rare springs which may be miles away. Barrels filled with water are hauled in wagons, sometimes for a distance of twenty miles. Today, the wagons are rapidly being replaced by pickup trucks, and, where, long ago, the horse changed Navaho life, now the automobile is bringing another great change. Water is still scarce, but both the tribal government and the Indian Service are developing new wells, bringing some relief from the long hauls that have been necessary for too many years. Water is still conserved to the utmost. Once, when we were visiting under a summer shelter, our friend Paulina was making ready to wash a few dishes. I asked her if I might make a picture showing how the Navaho can wash dishes in a tea cup full of water. She took me quite literally and, measuring out a cup, proceeded to wash the few dishes. And they were clean. It is surprising how cool it can be under one of these shelters on a hot summer day, for there is always a breeze—all one needs is shade.

In the summer of 1954 we made a trip to the Navaho Mountain area in southeastern Utah. This is still a

(OPPOSITE) *Interior of horizontal log hogan in the Cove Area.*

*Washing dishes under a brush shelter.*

remote region, one containing much old Navaho life. We spent a memorable day with the family of Old Lady Long Salt at her summer hogan. Through our interpreter, who was her great granddaughter-in-law, she told us something of her long life. She was eight years old when the Navaho People returned from the Long Walk, and she told us of hardships they had endured, the effort of starting life again on their old homesites, and the fight for survival.

The shelter of Old Lady Long Salt was a natural one, for here low cedar and juniper trees grew in a circle. There was the same pattern of entrance and placement of objects as in a winter hogan. Over the loom area and where the family slept, canvasses had been hung for protection from summer rain storms. *[See pp. 70–71.]* We were soon to learn, to our astonishment, that we were in the presence of five generations of daughters. The Old Lady (94, we figured, and still vigorous) sits at the extreme left of this picture; directly behind her, our interpreter; making kneel-down bread near the fire is the Old Lady's daughter; beyond the Old Lady, looking at my book of pictures,

*The summer hogan of Old Lady Long Salt.*

SALT

*A Navaho costume of the 1880's.*

are her granddaughter and great-granddaughter. The little girl in the center is the great great-granddaughter.

The sons and grandsons were away at work, and sons-in-law would never be there, for the old rule still is imposed in most areas, that a man must never speak to his mother-in-law. We spent several hours visiting this family. They were interested in us and in the things we observed. They looked at every picture in my book with the greatest of interest, pointing out differences in costume, ornaments, or possessions. We watched the making of kneel-down bread—green corn cut from the cob, put through a meat grinder, salted, packed into the green husks, and baked in an outdoor oven. It was very good. We have found when visiting families such as this, that a time comes when their courtesy to us has been fulfilled, their curiosity is satisfied, and their normal work must be resumed. It is well to be sensitive to this approaching moment and to take one's leave before wearing out a welcome.

At Navaho Mountain we found a distinct difference in costume from that of other parts of the reservation, such as a broader collar on the women's blouses, different stitching, different use of silver buttons. Later, we were to learn that many areas have distinctive identifying stitching on the sleeves of the women's blouses. Before the days of American Occupation, the old apparel consisted (for the women) of two handwoven mantas (rectangular pieces of cloth) secured at each shoulder and tied about the waist with a woven belt. When the women saw the pioneer white women's long cotton dresses of the 1870–1880 period, such as those worn by the Army officers' wives at Bosque Redondo, they copied them, though they quickly made adaptations to suit their own needs, eliminating the tight bodices and substituting loose, comfortable blouses. At present there is a change from the cotton skirt, worn for so long a time, to one of rayon and similar material, and shorter in length. When C. N. Cotton introduced Pendleton blankets around the 1890's, their use as wearing apparel was quickly adopted, the men wearing the full blankets, the women the large fringed shawls.

Many of the Navaho People who come closest in contact with us, and who now speak English fluently, are wearing clothes like ours. However, velveteen blouses are still widely worn, with a great variety of bright colors, still decorated with silver buttons and

*Tying a "chongo."*

with belts of silver *conchas*[1] strung on leather. For a long time dimes and quarters to which silver loops had been soldered were also used as buttons, but these are fast disappearing. Some men and women still wear moccasins. All but gone is the old-type man's costume, which consisted of white cotton pants, velveteen blouse, and much silver ornamentation. Strings of turquoise, shell, coral, and silver beads are still worn by both men and women, no matter what the costume. Silk scarf headbands and Stetson hats are worn by the men and boys, while the women wear scarfs or fringed Pendleton shawls.

The family is very important to all Navaho People. They are proud of having many relations. There are today more than sixty clans, groups of related people. Lineage is traced through the mother, and a son or daughter must marry outside his or her clan. Marriages are usually arranged by family or relatives when a boy or a girl reaches the proper age. A dowry of sheep or horses, or other items is presented by the family of the boy. Navaho relationships are hard for us to understand, for the Navaho have other words, or groups of words, for aunts, uncles, cousins, and

[1] *Concha* ("shell" in Spanish) is used by the Navaho to denote a shell-like medallion.

other relatives. I have heard Navaho people speak of "my uncle," only to find quite a different relationship from our knowledge of the word. A true uncle is spoken of as "my mother's brother," for instance.

Of the approximately twelve hundred Indian languages of the Americas, certain linguistic interrelationships have been described and established by scholars. In addition, many dialects still exist within the languages spoken by closely related tribes.

Navaho origins lie in a hypothetical group—the Nadene people—who are believed to have migrated to Alaska from Asia centuries ago, and who branched into four major language families, one of which is Athabascan. These Athabascan-speaking people gradually migrated over a wide expanse of territory stretching from Alaska to Mexico, some following along the Pacific Coast, others following along the Rocky Mountains. There are many sub-groups and offshoots even of the Athabascan, one such subgroup being the Apache from whom the Navaho are an offshoot.

The Navaho language is not a "primitive" form of expression but is a highly complex form of communication. Differing greatly from English and other European tongues, it is a language full of movement, of subtle meaning, of verbs whose action may be modified by a wide variety of prefixes.

Some scholars believe that there is a relationship between the ancient language of the Nadene and the Chinese-Tibetan languages, and, though the rela-

*Timothy's mother, who lives near Lukachukai.*

*Washburn Begay's hogan on the mountain.*

tionship is probable, much more research is needed to establish it as a fact. Like the Chinese languages, Navaho is a "tone language," and the meaning of the words is distinguished by the pitch of the voice, whether it be raised or lowered.

Navaho is a difficult language for English-speaking people to learn, and many of the sounds are very hard for us to produce, yet there are many who have accomplished this feat. Mr. Robert Young, area tribal operations officer of the Bureau of Indian Affairs in Gallup, is one of those who has gained exceptional proficiency in the language. He has traveled in Western Canada, including British Columbia, where there are other Athabascan-speaking people, with whom he had no difficulty in establishing a working relationship. Though the Athabascan languages have become too divergent over the centuries to be mutually intelligible, there are enough similarities in vocabulary, structure, and other features to demonstrate their close relationship. The people with whom he worked in the north were as interested in the Navaho language as he was in theirs.

In addition to a dictionary and grammar, Mr. Young has written an extensive article in the *Navajo*

*Yearbook* (1961),[2] focused especially on the problems of teaching English to Navaho beginners. It has sufficient detail to give insight into the grammatical structure and sound system of the language for those who seek some knowledge of the Navaho tongue.

One summer while I was working in the Red Rock area, Betsy and I heard about a road over the top of the Lukachukai Mountains which led to the trading post of Toadlena on the eastern slope of the mountains. Deciding to explore this, we started on the old road that crossed the mountains to the post of Lukachukai on the western slope. As we reached the top we found the branch road leading south. At first it was almost impassable, and at one extremely rough and steep point I remarked, as we started a third attempt, "If we don't make it this time, we'll go back." Fortunately we did make it and soon we were driving through a beautiful pine and spruce forest with occasional groves of aspen.

As we rounded a bend, before us on a rise a little above the road level was a beautiful log hogan, built

[2] "A Sketch of the Navajo Language," *The Navajo Yearbook*, pp. 430–510.

in a small clearing, the pines and spruces towering beyond. Sitting outside busy at their work were two women and a small child, the elder woman carding wool, the younger grinding corn on an old-type metate.[3] They seemed surprised that a car had come from the northerly direction, but greeted us as we approached. We found that neither of the women spoke English, so in a little while I produced my book of pictures and soon they were engrossed in looking at them. Then I heard an exclamation of "Mamma, Mamma!"—it seemed that I had photographed the older woman's mother at some distant point. I took the print out of the book and gave it to her, to her delight. After a while I asked if I might make some more pictures (sign language) and, receiving a nod of acquiescence, I set to work. We spent the rest of the morning with these people and, as noon approached, we packed up and were ready to continue our journey.

*I make a baby-board for you, my son.*
*May you grow to a great old age.*
*Of the rays of the earth I make the back,*
*The blanket, I make of the black clouds,*
*The bow, I make of the rainbow,*
*The side-loops, I make of the sun beams,*
*The foot board, I make of the sun-dogs,*
*The covering, I make of the dawn,*
*The bed, I make of the black fog.*

*[This prayer is sung when a baby is placed on the cradleboard.]*

Suddenly we heard it—a Navaho song—soaring from the woods in the clear, silent mountain air. It was a song of utter joy, of complete freedom of spirit, such as I had never heard. We stood spellbound. Soon there was added the tinkle of sheep bells as out of the forest they all came, the sheep, the man, his little son, and a dog. The shepherd stopped abruptly when he saw strangers and a veil came down like the dropping of a curtain at the theatre. He approached slowly, greeting us with usual Navaho courtesy. But in those first few unguarded moments we had glimpsed the Navaho soul. Soon we were on our way, enriched beyond measure by this experience.

We never did find the road to Toadlena; we came out at Sanostee instead. But what matter?

The Navaho have songs of many kinds. There are sacred songs, the chants from the many ceremonies, hundreds of them. There are songs for an individual, songs for chorus. A medicine man must know all the chants in every ceremony he conducts. There are songs related to all forms of living creatures, songs of protection, songs to ward off evil. There are songs for daily activities, there are songs about sacred mountains and places. There are songs of sorrow, songs of gladness, songs of supplication. There are songs for games, songs for pleasure. A Navaho feels rich according to how many songs he knows. There are songs for smaller ceremonies, songs for the blessing of a new hogan, a song for the building of a baby's cradleboard.

Fastened to the bow of the cradleboard there is always a charm to ward off evil—a piece of turquoise or shell. In some localities there are "lucky" cradle-

[3] A stone slab with a concave upper surface.

*Watching her grandchild.*

boards. When a mother has raised a particularly strong and healthy baby, other expectant mothers want to borrow the cradleboard, so that their children, too, may be strong and healthy. The Navaho themselves believe that the use of the cradleboard produces strong and straight backs in their children, and that the security of being bound onto the board tends to produce a calm and poised personality.

The Navaho have a different attitude toward children from ours. Children, even small ones, are treated as little people and learn to make their own decisions at an early age.

*Trading Posts*

When the Navaho returned from Fort Sumner to that portion of their old land allotted them by the treaty of 1868, trading posts were soon to play a vital role in their lives. By the early 1870's Mormon traders were coming down from Utah establishing contacts for trade at the San Juan and Colorado rivers. John D. Lee, in 1874, initiated a ferry which crossed the Colorado not many miles above the Grand Canyon. Here also he established a post, one of the first to deal directly with the Navaho, where he traded horses for the fine hand-woven blankets made by the Navaho women. These lovely blankets were rapidly coming into great demand among the Mormons of Utah. Long in use, Lee's Ferry was not abandoned until 1926 when the Navaho Bridge, built at this site, linked the Navaho country with north central Arizona and southern Utah.

Licensed by the government agent at Fort Defiance, traders began to appear as the Navaho produced wool and blankets. Few in number at the beginning, the traders increased in proportion to the volume of Navaho production. Strict rules of trade were imposed by the government when licenses were issued, and, with but few exceptions, the traders never owned the land upon which their posts were built.

The pioneer trader was a rugged individual, able to survive in remote areas under the most primitive conditions. He had to build what he needed, had to be able to fix anything and everything, and through the years has taught necessary construction and mechanical techniques to many Navaho. Built of stone, adobe bricks, or, occasionally, logs, the old trading posts consisted of one or more buildings, with sheep and horse corrals nearby. In addition to the store, there was usually a barn, a storehouse, and a visitors' hogan for the use of Indians who lived far away. Around three walls of the post were shelves reaching to the ceiling, stocked with goods of all descriptions. In front of the shelves, and separated from them by a passageway, were high, wide counters, built so for protection as well as use. Beneath the counters were shelves for an assortment of articles, tools, and, in early days, a weapon or two in case of need. In the center of the room, or to one side, a large old-fashioned iron stove gave warmth in winter, and along the remaining wall were benches to accommodate the customers. Hanging from the ceiling were coils of rope, lanterns, buckets, bridles, harnesses, and other items of trade. For sixty years many trading posts were in isolated spots, far removed from worldly contact. The few roads, usually bad ones, were often impossible to travel at certain times of year. Horse- or mule-drawn wagons were the only means of carrying supplies or delivering goods for sale.

Many legendary personalities were among those early traders on the reservation: Keam, the Hubbells, the Wetherills, the Hyde brothers (who were the first to send hides to the eastern market), C. N. Cotton, who saw a potential market for rugs in the east, Sam Day, "Cozy" McSparron, B. I. Staples, both Charles and Arthur Newcomb, Bruce Bernard, and others whose names were synonymous with the posts they held. Off the reservation there were the Kirks, the Fred Harvey Company, and a few others.

The traders' abilities were legion. They had to speak a most difficult language, they had to be shrewd business men in order to exist, and they had to be pioneers in every sense of the word. As the Navaho of these early times seldom had cash with which to make their purchases, a credit barter system was devised whereby a Navaho could place certain items of his possession, chiefly his jewelry, in pawn until that time of year when wool or sheep were sold.

Each trading post was, and still is, a center, like the hub of a wheel, the outer circumference being perhaps twenty or more miles away. To these posts the Navaho have been coming to trade for nearly a hundred years, bringing their produce to exchange for goods they desire or need. They bring wool at shearing time, sheep and some cattle at fall roundup time,

*The trading post at Shonto is nestled in a small canyon of red sandstone. The post building, at the extreme left, is nearly surrounded by fine trees. The large hogan-shaped buildings at the right are the Shonto day school.*

*In those areas on the reservation where piñon trees abound, the Navaho gather the nuts to sell to the trader. Piñon nuts, though small, are very sweet and delicious, and are a substantial side crop for the People.*

*The old trading post at Red Rock has undergone several remodelings. Built of stone, its exterior walls have in recent years been plastered, and the interior modernized. The nice old barn was torn down several years ago.*

*In 1932 the Red Rock trading post still had its original dirt floor.*

and hides, piñon nuts, handmade jewelry, woven blankets, and rugs throughout the year. The trading post has become a place of meeting, as well as the place to obtain water, for all posts had to be built where there were natural springs or good wells. The trader has been the connecting link between the United States government and the Navaho People. The trading post is where government officials come to set dates for spring branding and dipping of sheep, to announce farm demonstrations, and to post notices. It is the trader who interprets government regulations and who makes contacts between the government officials and the individual Navaho of his region. And it has been the trader who has established outside markets for rugs and jewelry. By and large, the trader has been the best friend the Navaho have had over a long period of time. It has been to the trader that the Navaho have gone for help in time of need, for many a trader has driven miles in good weather or bad, by day or night, to take sick Navaho People to the nearest hospital. There have been a few exceptions where exploitation or unfairness in trade have taken place, but such traders soon disappeared, for the shrewd Navaho quickly detect these practices and simply go elsewhere for their business.

During the past thirty years road improvement has progressed with increasing rapidity, until today new paved roads link the major sections of the reservation.

*In the warehouse at Red Rock, the trader stacks hides and wool. Here trader Troy Kennedy is examining wool for its quality and cleanliness.*

*Filling water barrels at the Valley Store.*

*Women returning from a trip to the trading post.*

Distances seem to have shrunk, as trucks now travel one hundred miles in two hours, where not long ago the same trip took two days.

The trader's influence has been great, depending on the way he has conducted his business, his attitude to his customers, and his interest in them and their mode of life. In all activities, both in the store and out, the trader's actions are observed and noted. He must be ever on the alert for values, for the Navaho loves the game of trading and trying to get the best of any bargain. Spending time in a trading post, watching the comings and goings of the many people who appear daily; is a fascinating experience. Navaho People come into the post, quietly greet those they know by a gentle touching of hands, then sit on the benches for a long time considering what to buy. One will finally go up to the counter, and, pointing to an article, put down the money for that one item, or if the Navaho is pawning jewelry, the trader lists each purchase. Following another long interlude of consideration, this procedure will be repeated. Sometimes individuals will stay at the post all day before the final lot of merchandise has been acquired. Always there is the purchase of tobacco (in early times there was a box of loose tobacco on the counter for free samples), and the purchase of candy or pop for children, as the day proceeds. The Navaho observe everything, listen to all conversations, deliberate. When they go home they will remember everything that has transpired.

In every post there is a special place, sometimes a vault, often a small room, where pawned jewelry is kept. Items are ticketed with the owner's name, the date, and the amount owed. Most traders keep jewelry in pawn longer than the legal time of three years for the owner to redeem it (though this has recently been changed). Then it may be placed in a case as "dead pawn" for sale to any who will buy. The traders are more than fair about this transaction. I recall an instance when I had been requested to buy some dead pawn for a shop. One piece was a particularly fine *concha* belt. It had been dead pawn for over three years. Six weeks after I had bought it, the original owner rode more than fifty miles to redeem his belt. He was crestfallen to find it gone. The trader took the time and trouble to write requesting its return. Fortunately, it had not been sold and the Navaho redeemed his prized possession.

Probably the least changed of the famous trading posts is the Hubbell Post at Ganado, Arizona.[4] This is one of the exceptions where the land was homesteaded by Don Lorenzo Hubbell, for at that time, 1876, this land was not part of the reservation. Don Lorenzo, the son of a Connecticut Yankee and a Spanish mother, purchased a store built six years previously at this site, in all probability the oldest post following the first at Fort Defiance. When Don Lorenzo bought the post, he also homesteaded a 160-acre tract of land. He erected a number of fine substantial buildings during the course of his life. His post became a mecca for anthropologists, archaeologists, writers, and a host of visitors, as did the posts of other famous traders.

Here, in Don Lorenzo's treasure room, is his late son Roman Hubbell, discussing the merits of a rug just brought in to be sold. On the walls are hung relics of the past—Kit Carson's gun scabbard, a fine old gun collection, water containers of many different types, a superb collection of Indian baskets from various tribes, archaeological specimens from nearby early Pueblo ruins. Piled high along another wall of the room are stacks of Navaho rugs, all of top quality, for which the Hubbell Post has always been famous. "Cozy" McSparron, Hubbell, and later the Lippincotts at Wide Ruins, did much to restore the use of natural dyes in rug making. This is one of many instances when the traders' influence has counted most, and today certain areas of the reservation are noted for rugs of widely different types.

Other traders whose interests lay beyond the trading counter were John Wetherill at Kayenta, Sam Day, B. I. Staples at Coolidge, J. B. Moore at Crystal, and the Newcombs, to name but a few. Harry Goulding at Monument Valley has done much to promote the scenic beauty of his area. At Shiprock, Bruce Bernard has one of the finest pawn rooms, with an excellent system for recording the pawn. His room is a spectacle of turquoise, coral, and silver. The wives of these traders also have played an important role in their respective areas, teaching many useful household arts, aiding families, and learning much of the Navaho ways. The heyday of these posts is gone now, and modernization is rapidly taking over, though

[4] Now to be a national monument.

*Charles Dickens marking jewelry in the pawn room of the Bruce Bernard Trading Post.*

*Roman Hubbell in his trading post.*

there are still a few smaller posts in remote areas retaining some of the flavor of the early years. It will not be long before these, too, are changed, and with their passing will go one of the most colorful phases of Western history, one so closely bound to the Navaho that it became a part of the Way of the People.

Away from the well-traveled highways, old methods of locomotion still are used. For three hundred years the horse has been a dearly loved possession. When a Navaho dies, his horse is shot and the saddle is buried with the man. A Navaho thinks nothing of walking many miles if he has no means of transportation. We have come upon this many times. Once, as we were traveling to Tuba City from the Hopi country, we came to a slight crest in the undulating desert; beyond we saw a family—a woman with a baby in a cradleboard and a small child riding a burro, while two older boys were on foot. When we reached them we produced some candy for the children and tried to chat a little, though no one seemed to understand

English. They were curious about us, surprised by our offer, and thoroughly friendly. They seemed miles from any habitation, yet in the gentle rise and fall of the desert, it is remarkable how a hogan can be hidden from view.

Another time, as we drove along in the Red Rock region, we came across a boy with a small flock of sheep. It was a wonderful day with great masses of clouds gathering for a possible storm. We pulled off the road to stop a while to enjoy the beauty of the scene. Soon the sheep came closer to us, the boy watching from a distance. We were so absorbed with this scene in one direction that we did not see a young man approaching on foot from another. Then up out of a wash appeared a lone horseman who stopped to talk with the young man on foot. After a while each went his separate way as we watched them all disappear into the landscape. The sheep moved slowly on, the little boy with them. We spoke to no one, they paid no attention to us whatsoever, yet I doubt not that later in the day they knew who we were and a surprising lot about us.

*The little shepherd.*

*During a long drought this boy brought his sheep eight miles to the nearest water.*

*Bringing home a flock of sheep on a windy day.*

*The nutritious grama grass of the West.*

*Flocks of sheep are gathered prior to shipping to market.*

*Sheep Raising*

Ever since the Navaho obtained their first sheep and horses from the Spaniards sometime in the seventeenth century, sheep and wool have become an ever increasing resource for the People. Between that time and the year 1846, when the United States took possession of the Southwest following the Mexican War, Navaho sheep had increased to 500,000 head. Later, when Kit Carson defeated the Navaho through his scorched-earth policy, much of this livestock was captured or killed. Only some 5,000 head were moved to Fort Sumner with the Navaho People; many of these died along the way, for they had not sufficient time to graze, and more died later.

When at last the Navaho were freed to return to their old land in 1868, they had nothing but the hope of the promised new start that the government would send them—seed, tools, and three sheep per family. It was more than a year, a time of near starvation, before this promise was fulfilled. Before the exile there had been some small groups who, with their flocks, had hidden in the remote wild canyons of northern Arizona, while Colonel Carson was rounding up the Tribe. There is a legend that one leader of the hidden groups urged the People to conserve their sheep so that they might help their fellow tribesmen when the day of liberation came. Doubtless some of the re-

*Sheep being brought to trading post.*

turning Navaho found their way to these remote regions, joining their relatives or friends. The rest struggled through that first year until the promised sheep and seed were finally delivered late in the fall of 1869.

By the year 1870 there could not have been many sheep on the reservation, yet between 1870 and 1894 sheep and other stock had increased to an estimated number of more than 1,500,000. During these first years following the exile, government agents were sent to certain areas on the reservation to maintain contact with the Navaho People. The first agent to realize the necessity for stock reduction was D. M. Riordan, agent at Fort Defiance, who sent a report to Washington requesting that the stock on the reservation be reduced, and also urging the introduction of better stock to improve the breed. This was in 1883. Again, in 1894, another agent, Edwin Plummer, realizing the great increase in stock, particularly of sheep, sent an urgent plea to Washington for more grazing land for the Navaho, but this plea also was turned aside. The next important effort to intercede in behalf of the Navaho was in 1914 by Father Anselm Weber from St. Michael's Mission. Father Anselm became aroused when a group of non-Indian stockmen, with eyes on certain grazing areas, tried to bring political pressure to bear on the Indian Service to declare this large section of land, then beyond the western boundary of the reservation, as "surplus land," and, therefore, part of the public domain and subject to homesteads.

Father Anselm attacked this measure, sending reports to Washington showing the need for increased areas for the Navaho. Riordan, Plummer, and Father Anselm were the first who realized how the pasturage was being destroyed by over-grazing, who recognized the danger of the destruction of the natural grama grass so necessary for stock of all kinds. Father Anselm saw, too, how certain areas of land were being eroded where the sheep, who crop closely and often pull up the grass by the roots, were actually destroying the range. He urged Congress not only to preserve the Navaho range lands, but also to increase range areas. Father Anselm was successful in his mission, and new areas of land were added to the western section of the reservation. However, nothing was done about the overstocked range.

Following World War I, there was much discussion about the land and the sheep, but no one seemed to have any plan. Finally, in 1930, an Indian Bureau forester, William H. Zeh, was appointed to make a general survey of range conditions on the whole reservation. Mr. Zeh's report showed that due to shortage of stock water the distribution of stock was very uneven. Consequently, there were great inroads of soil erosion in some areas, and stock of all kinds—sheep, horses, cattle, mules, burros, and goats—were far in excess of the available range. He urged a stock reduction program. Once more there were delays and the detailed grazing surveys were not commenced until 1933, to be completed in 1935. It was then apparent that the reservation range could support only about 500,000 head, and that the range at that time was overstocked by more than 200 percent. These were the depression years and the price of wool and lambs was at a low point. The Navaho were just not selling their lambs, thereby adding still more stock to the overgrazed land.

With the advent of the new administration in 1932, new agencies were created, the Soil Conservation Service, the Public Works Program, the Relief Administration, to name a few. These services, together with the reports from the Indian Service, brought to focus the necessity for the Navaho stock reduction program of the 1932–1942 decade. This program produced an economic and social revolution, for the Navaho at that time did not have the education or the understanding to comprehend the necessity for this long-range plan. To a people who had been shepherds for more than two centuries, to be told that they must reduce their flocks came as a shock.

Until this time the Navaho had had no centralized government of their own. In the early days before the exile they had been loosely governed by chiefs in various areas of the Navaho country. After the exile the Indian Service had divided the reservation into districts of administration. Now, in 1932, the tribal government was just being formulated, and still did not represent the people from all the areas of the reservation. The first steps taken by the new commissioner of Indian affairs were in the field of land conservation, to be carried out by the Public Works Program, giving work to many Navaho men. Steps also were taken to develop greater water supply by drilling new wells and building small drainage reservoirs.

Then came the time when the whole land and sheep

*The ever increasing use of trucks and cars is fast diminishing the use of the long-loved horse.*

program was clearly stated and explained to the Tribal Council, showing them how too many sheep were destroying the grass and causing great areas of extreme erosion. To compensate for the reduction in sheep, a new educational program would be put into effect which would include the building of some fifty new day schools. The construction of these buildings would be done by Navaho labor. The Council understood the program and approved it. Work was commenced. The Relief Administration was to purchase 100,000 head of sheep immediately in the fall of 1933, this number to be divided among the several jurisdictions of the reservation.

But many of the large sheep owners refused to comply. A compromise was finally reached on a percentage basis, but this worked hardships on the small flock owners. Suspicion and resentment reached a high pitch, for the Navaho think of wealth in terms of livestock, not money, and they seemed unable to understand that money earned by wages would in any way compensate for loss of sheep. While the Council supported the program, enforcing it was something else, and the Council was placed in a difficult position with their fellow Navaho who disapproved the plan. There were several years of turmoil, climaxed when the Relief Administration purchased 150,000 head of goats, half of them females. At this point the Navaho women became very agitated and hostile to the entire program. These goats were to be delivered to small packing plants between September and December of 1934, with a purchase price of $1.00 per head. Unusual weather conditions and long distances for hauling slowed the program, and a suggestion was made that the Navaho slaughter all the goats they could use for food, even though they had already been sold to the government.

Frustrated in getting some 3,500 of these goats to the railroad from one far distant point, and because the cost of hauling greatly exceeded the value of the animals, someone ordered that the goats be shot and left to rot. This action may have been a practical solution, but its effect on the Navaho was catastrophic and sent a shudder of apprehension throughout the Tribe, for, to the Navaho, animals are killed only for food. This was a tragedy which has left scars of mistrust, and even though the program was continued and the stock reduced to a better level, sheep control is still a matter of concern. In continuing the program, range management districts have been established, while the Bureau of Indian Affairs still issues the grazing permits.

The coming of World War II alleviated the tension to a considerable extent, for many Navaho men went into the army, many more, and women also, into war work of various kinds. Some went to California to work in defense plants. They all did a superlative job. These war experiences also taught the Navaho a great deal about the ways of other people, for they are quick to learn through observation, and to many this was a new experience, for they had never been away from the reservation. Following the war many more things have happened to help relieve the livestock situation. The discovery of extensive uranium deposits brought money into the Tribal Fund, as well as work for many young men. This discovery was followed by the development of new oil fields. The Tribal Council is doing much to produce new water supplies, build new roads, and carry out other projects, all of which are helping to solve Navaho economic life. While there are still many sheep on the reservation, they are no longer the only means of livelihood.

*Farming*

The Navaho have been farmers since the beginning of their known history. Evidence of their produce was found in archaeological excavations in old Navaholand where corn, squash, and beans were found—seeds more than four hundred years old. As the Navaho moved westward down the San Juan Valley, they planted fields wherever they settled, but these were subsistence farms of small acreage. During the past seventy-five years, this picture has been changing, until today there are some Navaho who do practice commercial farming, and there are more who wish to do so.

As about 65 percent of land under irrigation on the reservation at the moment is concentrated in the San Juan Valley, a farm training program was established in this area by the government about ten or more years ago, to meet the need for new occupations to take the place of raising sheep. As this has developed, the Navaho have found that small subsistence acreage would not meet their needs, and as this need has increased, a consolidation of small areas has been developed, making productive farming as a livelihood more possible.

The new irrigation project, planned long ago but not put into effect until 1962, will bring water from the San Juan River, stored in the new Navajo Reservoir, to irrigate 110,000 acres of land. This area, now nearly destitute of growth, will extend along the south side of the river from near Farmington, south and west all the way to Newcomb. The first water will be turned into the new canals in a few years, creating about one thousand 120-acre farms for young Navaho People. This project is based on the premise that the land belongs to the Tribe and will be leased to individuals with a period of rent-free occupancy in which to become established. Farming on a commercial basis is a comparatively new occupation for the Navaho, and benefits from the farm training program will be needed as this development gets under way.

Although Indians in this part of the Southwest have

*Navaho fences have very ingenious construction. Utilizing the natural crotches in piñon and cedar trees, a fence will be built by entwining cross pieces in the crotches. Such a fence is built without a nail, wire, or any fastening whatever. It simply holds itself up. It is sturdy and will last for years.*

*The Nakai family with a crop of melons on the bank of the San Juan River.*

*An irrigator turning water from a new source onto previously unbroken soil.*

*Irrigating a newly plowed field.*

*Winnowing beans on a small farm.*

*Agricultural exhibit at the Shiprock Fair.*

*Drying freshly cut alfalfa.*

practiced irrigation since the twelfth century or before, the modern refinements in head gates, and water storage have so increased production that they have brought about a decided change in Navaho life. The change from subsistence to commercial productivity is great, but here, once more, the native adaptability of the Navaho will serve him in good stead.

*The Landscape*

Navaholand abounds in interesting sites, as well as scenic beauty. Adjacent to the reservation are three national parks and seven national monuments. The Grand Canyon, Petrified Forest, and Mesa Verde National Parks are all in close proximity, as are the national monuments of Walnut Canyon, Sunset Crater, and Wupatki to the west, El Morro (Inscription Rock) to the south, and Hovenweep and Aztec Ruins to the north. Within the reservation are four more—Rainbow Bridge, Canyon de Chelly, Chaco Canyon, and Navajo National Monuments—with the recent addition of the Navaho Tribal Park at Monument Valley, developed and operated by the Tribe with uniformed personnel, who are graduates of the National Park Service Ranger Training School. Plans are



*The first appointed Navaho to the National Park Service staff, serving as a ranger at Navajo National Monument, was Hubert Laughter. Today he is a member of the Tribal Council.*

*The ancient cliff dwelling of Beta-ta-kin in the Navajo National Monument.*

under way for several more additions to the tribal park system.

Chaco Canyon Monument and Navajo National Monument contain great prehistoric ruins indicating the extensive population that existed here between the eleventh and fourteenth centuries, and there are other sites antedating these. The ruins of the great terraced structures of Pueblo Bonito and Chetro Ketl at Chaco Canyon reveal some of the finest prehistoric masonry. Here one sees the remains of two walled cities where perhaps a thousand people lived nine hundred years ago, and there are ruins of many other pueblos within this area. Navajo National Monument contains the cliff dwelling called Beta-ta-kin, perhaps the most beautiful in the Southwest, as well as other ruins. Canyon de Chelly and its tributary, Canyon del Muerto, comprise the most spectacular monument for scenic beauty. Here is an area of long-continued occupation, seventeen centuries, from A.D. 200 to the present. Not only do these Canyons contain evidences of ancient habitation, but through all these centuries the canyon floors have been farmed by successive tribes of Indians.

First came the so-called Basket Makers of A.D. 200 to approximately 700, followed by the Pueblos, who built the famous White House in Canyon de Chelly, the cliff dwellings in Mummy and Massacre Caves, and others in Canyon del Muerto. Then, according to some archaeologists, came some Hopi, who left behind quantities of pottery in the thirteenth and fourteenth centuries.

Lastly came the Navaho in the early part of the eighteenth century. This is still an inhabited region, for some three hundred Navaho live and raise their crops within the Canyons, sheltered by their high protective walls. As visitors travel up the Canyons today, they are conscious of small farms of corn and alfalfa, but it is only from the air that the full extent of the farming may be seen.

Throughout the summer, irrigating ditches bring water from higher regions as it flows down the Canyons following heavy thunderstorms. There are small peach orchards in Canyon del Muerto whose origins stem from trees brought to the Hopi villages by seventeenth-century Spanish padres. In September the Navaho dry large quantities of peaches to be stored for winter use.

There has long been misunderstanding regarding the names of these canyons, De Chelly, and its largest tributary, Del Muerto. *De Chelly* is a Spanish corruption of the Navaho word *Tseghi*, meaning "between the rocks," hence, canyon. Many have thought that the name *Del Muerto* came from the Spanish attack on Massacre Cave in 1804, but there is no evidence whatever that this branch canyon had any name until 1882 when Colonel James Stevenson entered the canyon on an archaeological expedition. Members of two earlier expeditions made no mention of any name other than De Chelly. In a cave, later called Mummy Cave, Colonel Stevenson found two mummies, and in recognition of this find, he called the canyon "Cañon de los Muertos," later condensed to Canyon del Muerto.[5]

The Canyons can be treacherous as well as beautiful. Few visitors realize how quickly water can accumulate following the great thunderstorms of this Western region. Sometimes a storm will be miles away, not even visible from the lower part of the Canyons; yet with incredible speed the runoff accumulates, rushing down the Canyon floors, sweeping everything in its path. There are areas of quicksand, too, where many an automobile has become bogged down and even submerged, to the dismay of unsuspecting travelers. The Canyons twist and wind, creating one beautiful vista after another when the lowering light of afternoon mystifies and enhances, and giant shafts of rock, sunlit against a shadowed wall, are silhouetted in majestic beauty.

There is a delightful legend of how the Canyons were made:

> Coyote went to the People begging them to give him some fire. At first they refused, for he was well known as the mischief maker. After repeated entreaties, some one said, "Oh, give him some." So they gave him some flint stones. He tried and tried but could not make a spark. Finally he became angry and threw the stones on the ground, whereupon a great spark was lighted which quickly set fire to the dry brush. It burned and burned into a rushing fire and Coyote ran away. The earth split open from the great heat beneath the fire and finally Water Pourer came to put it out. This started the washing

[5] David L. DeHarport, "Origin of the Name, Cañon del Muerto," *El Palacio*, 67, No. 3 (June, 1960), 95.

*The upper end of Canyon de Chelly from the air.*

down of the Canyon walls, making them deeper and deeper. Today, when you stand on the rim you can see how the Canyons would all fit back together.[6]

In September of 1957 I made a special trip to Canyon de Chelly, taking with me Maria Teba, a young Navaho woman who was then working in Santa Fe, and whom Betsy and I knew very well. She had never been to the Canyons and was most eager to go, and I thought it delightful to have a Navaho companion. On the way we stopped at Window Rock, where I found the Tribal Council in session. I obtained permission to make some interior photographs of the Council room with the members present. I also made a portrait of Paul Jones, who was chairman at that time.

Proceeding on to Chinle, we put up our tent in the National Monument camp grounds and settled down for a stay of several days. One thing I wanted to do was hire the Jeep and its driver from the Thunderbird Ranch for a trip up Canyon del Muerto. As this was not possible for the following day, we made arrangements for the day after. We then rearranged our plans, driving up to Many Farms, some forty miles to the north, where Cornell University conducts a clinic. We spent a busy morning watching the school children as they came in for tests, making numerous pictures, and learning about the interesting work that is being carried out by this university.

At noon we started on our way back to camp. As we were passing a small trading post called the Valley Store, I realized suddenly that this was the old Frazier Trading Post, the end of my long walk in 1930 when Betsy and I ran out of gasoline. We stopped to buy something for lunch and to pass the time of day with the trader. As we started back to the car, a wagon drove up with a man and his wife coming to fill their water barrels. As this was an activity I had not yet photographed, I got out my hand camera, and, with Maria as interpreter, asked if I might make the picture I wanted. The man was willing, so I proceeded to make a number of exposures from different angles. After returning to the car, which was on the opposite side of the water tank, we drove for a short distance until we found a nice spot to stop for our lunch.

Then we returned to the Canyon and drove up on the rim to watch the sunset before going to our camp. After supper I got out my changing bag to reload my exposed film holders, and suddenly I could not find the case that contained all my small camera holders, as well as extra equipment. We hunted and hunted, ending by taking everything out of the car. It just wasn't there, so I assumed that I must have left it at the Many Farms Clinic. The next morning, having to postpone our trip up the Canyon, we drove all the way back to Many Farms. But the case wasn't there; we returned to the Valley Store, where I now knew I must have left it. Entering the store, we found only one man sitting there talking to the trader, who was busy behind his counter. I asked him if such a case had been found, thinking that I must have put it down somewhere and left it. He said he had not seen it or heard of it. Then the lone customer spoke in Navaho to Maria, telling her that he thought a certain young Navaho boy knew something about it. I realized then that it had been stolen, something that

[6] Adapted from Richard Van Valkenburgh, *Diné Bekéyah*, p. 22.

*Canyon de Chelly.*

*Many small farms cover the floor of Canyon del Muerto.*

*A corn field and hogan at the foot of soaring cliffs.*

*After a rain in Canyon de Chelly.*

*Canyon del Muerto joins Canyon de Chelly a short distance above the mouth.*

had happened to me only once before over the years. I posted a notice saying that it was lost and offering a reward. We returned to our camp to prepare for the trip up the Canyon the following day.

I was unhappy over the handicap I would have without the use of my hand camera, as all the extra film I had for it was in that case, including other accessories and a new exposure meter. But, of course, I had my large camera. We set forth early the following morning with the Jeep to ourselves and a nice Navaho driver. The floors of the Canyons are very treacherous with both dry sand and quicksand, and one must be accompanied by someone who knows the safe routes. Our driver, Art, lived up in Canyon del Muerto, and, as this was the Canyon we wanted to see, we proceeded on our way, stopping at Art's hogan, where he introduced us to his family and showed us a fine rug his mother was weaving.

It was a beautiful fall day and we took our time, stopping frequently to work or to look at whatever interested us. We passed numerous hogans, for this is the Canyon where many Navaho People live. We went all the way up to Mummy Cave, a cliff dwelling miles from the mouth of the Canyon. But just before we arrived at this spot we came to a group of hogans and, seeing several children running to meet us, Art stopped the car to give them candy we had brought along. In a few minutes two women appeared, one of them approaching Maria, saying to her in English, "Did you girls find the case you lost yesterday?" I was astonished at this, for we must have been about forty miles from the Valley Store. How could this news have reached these people in less than twenty-four hours, and how were we recognized? I did not have a camera visible and we were not in my own car. This was a striking instance of how news travels on the reservation and how carefully all strangers are observed.

We had our lunch in the shade of some beautiful pine trees across the Canyon from Mummy Cave, resting a while before starting on our return trip. About half way down the Canyon is a group of hogans, almost a community, called Standing Cow, so named for an early pictograph carved on the face of the Canyon wall above one of the hogans. Here we found a busy scene. When we had passed this point on our way up the Canyon in the morning, no one was visible. Now we found a group of Navaho women and children busily spreading out the season's crop of peaches to dry. They had swept an area clean of loose earth and were placing the halved peaches open side up to dry in the sun. We watched this activity for some time, Maria in continual conversation with the women and thoroughly enjoying herself. Finally we left, driving down the rest of the way as the late afternoon sun threw long shadows across the Canyon floor.

The next morning was Friday, the opening of the Window Rock Fair, so we broke camp and prepared to leave. We stopped at the trading post, as I wanted to tell Mr. Nelson about the loss of my case, in the event that any of the items showed up at his post. I bought some food for lunch and when I joined Maria at the car she was talking to two older Navaho People. She told me that these people wanted to know if we would take them to Window Rock. I said that we would be glad to, but that I wanted to go back to the Valley Store first to see if my case had been found. We all got in the car, the man riding on our camp beds in the back of the station wagon, the woman in front with Maria and me. Maria was engrossed in conversation and I soon realized that she was telling the woman about my missing case and also about my book, for she got it out to show the pictures. As neither of these people spoke any English, I had to guess what all the talk was about. There was no one around the Valley Store when we got there. I went inside to speak to the trader, but no sign of the case.

Getting back into the car, I started to turn around to head for the fair, inwardly bemoaning the loss of much valuable equipment, as well as the exposed negatives of Chairman Paul Jones and the Tribal Council. The woman spoke to Maria, asking me "to go around that hill where it would be quiet." I couldn't imagine what she wanted, but I have never failed to follow such a lead. We drove three or four miles to a place out of view of the highway, with not even a hogan in sight. Then she asked me to stop. She got out of the car, asking us to join her. She told Maria to put a rug down on the ground and asked me to get out a case like the one I had lost. I still couldn't imagine what this was all about, but I said nothing and followed directions. Maria told me to kneel down beside the woman. Then, to my complete surprise, she began a

*The White House cliff dwelling in Canyon de Chelly (1930).*

hand-trembling ceremony over me. Hand tremblers are diviners—diagnosticians—and they are sought out by the Navaho People to find lost articles.[7] I could see Maria in wide-eyed wonder as the woman proceeded with the ritual. I watched the shadow of the trembling hand and arm in front of me and listened to the incantation. This lasted about fifteen minutes. Then the woman spoke to Maria, telling her that three boys had taken the case from my car. I was not to worry, as nothing would be hurt. I was to come back to the store in four days—two boys would bring the case back. I thanked the hand trembler for her services and made a small donation. Then we all decided that it was lunch time, made some sandwiches, and had our lunch right there.

We drove on to Window Rock and, as we approached, Maria told me that our new friends wanted to go on in to Gallup. Since there was something about the car that needed fixing, I decided that we might just as well go into town and spend the night there. In Gallup we parted with these two, some 125 miles from the Valley Store. We never saw them again.

Saturday morning we returned to Window Rock and the fair, where we spent an interesting and busy day. Sunday, I took Maria back to Gallup to put her on the bus, for she had to return to her job the next morning. There was other work I had intended to do in the Shiprock area, but instead of taking the direct road north, I decided to go the long way around. I returned alone to Chinle, spending the night there. Monday morning, the fourth day, I went to the Valley Store. The trader said he did not have the case, but that two boys had just been there asking if the case had been found. I thought that they were probably seeing if the coast was clear, so I left the reward money and postage with the trader, and, knowing that they would recognize my car, I thought the best thing to do was to go on my way. A few days after I reached home, the case was returned, its contents complete and unharmed.

This was a most interesting experience, leaving many unanswered questions. I know that the hand trembler and her husband had spoken to no one but Maria and me from the time they got into the car at Chinle, until we left them in Gallup. There are many accounts of lost articles being found by hand tremblers. That there are Navaho People who have extrasensory perception has been noted many times by a number of people. Was my experience one of these? I wish I knew the answer.

[7] Hand trembling, one of the lesser rituals, is used to recover lost or stolen property, or to diagnose illness. For the latter, the ceremony is more elaborate, involving the sprinkling of pollen on the patient, the singing of special songs (always four in number), and the presentation of gifts to Gila Monster, to whom the ceremony belongs. It is believed that Gila Monster sees everything that occurs, and keeps track of the actions of all people. In the case of lost or stolen property the trembler's hand leads to the location of the property, or else the trembler hears the far-away voice of Gila Monster.

The Navaho name for this ritual is "To Search for Something without Looking." (See W. W. Hill, "The Hand Tremblers," *El Palacio*, 38 [March-April, 1935], 65.)

*Drying peaches in Canyon del Muerto.*

*Display of wool with native plants used for dyes.*

# THE CRAFTS

## *The Weavers*

THE RAISING OF SHEEP, the spinning of wool, and the weaving of textiles are age-old activities in most parts of the world where fabrics of great variety and use have been produced during many centuries. When the Spanish Conquistadores first came to the American Southwest in 1540, they brought with them the first sheep ever seen by the Indian inhabitants. To the surprise of the invaders they found cotton garments woven by Pueblo Indians, made on well-perfected looms of Indian origin. In later years archaeologists were to find scraps of woven cotton fabrics buried in prehistoric ruins whose dates go back to the fifth century A.D.

These first sheep brought by Coronado were used chiefly as food for his marching army, so that eventually they were all consumed. Later, when Don Juan de Oñate came up the Rio Grande Valley to colonize New Mexico, he also brought sheep for domestic use. These animals were the common Spanish breed known as the *churro*. The Pueblo Indians soon learned the use of wool, and, as production of sheep spread, the western Pueblo Indians of the Zuñi and Hopi villages soon were weaving woolen garments.

At the time of the Great Rebellion of 1680, when all the Pueblo People united to drive the Spanish from their land, some groups, fearing the return of the Spanish soldiers, took refuge in Old Navaholand. In this region archaeologists, those intrepid investigators of ancient human habitation, have found remains of Pueblo dwellings in close proximity to those of Navaho origin, indicating an early association of the two Indian cultures. As the Navaho moved westward in the early 1700's, they encountered the Hopi in Canyon de Chelly and at the villages farther west. Possibly because of this close proximity of the two distinctly different Indian groups, many students of Indian culture in the Southwest have believed that the Navaho learned the art of weaving from the Pueblo people. However, recent research is pointing more and more to the probability that the Navaho brought the knowledge of weaving with them when they migrated to the Southwest. During these travels and sojourns they came through country where other Indian tribes were already spinning and weaving, and it is quite possible that the Navaho learned to make and to use the spindle and the loom long before they entered the area where they now live.

Had the Navaho learned from the Pueblo weavers, they would probably have used the same techniques, but they do not. Pueblo looms are stationary, whereas Navaho looms are portable. The spindles are different, and the use of them most distinctively so. Among the Navaho it has always been the women who are the weavers (with a few rare exceptions), while among the Pueblo, the weavers are usually men. Pueblo weavers are dominated by traditional forms and designs with little variation, while Navaho weavers are emphatically creative. Although it is true that traders of many areas have in recent years influenced types and designs of rugs to some extent, within these bounds there is great creativity. Over the long years of production from Navaho looms, the infinite variety of design, color, and weaving patterns has stamped the Navaho as masters of their art.

Navaho weavers have never changed in their use of the upright loom, nor have they made any change in its construction. The Spanish settlers in the Rio Grande Valley brought with them from Europe the knowledge of the treadle loom, which they built here of native woods, but the Navaho have steadfastly continued to use the upright aboriginal invention.

While the earliest examples of Navaho weaving have long since disappeared, there are references to this craft contained in letters from a number of Spanish writers. These remarks, together with their dates, are interesting indeed. One early letter of 1780 says, "The Navahos, who although of Apache kinship, have a fixed home, sow, raise herds, and weave their blankets and clothes of wool . . ."[1] The same Spaniard, Teodoro de Croix, fifteen years later refers to the Navaho: "The Navaho Nation has 700 families, more or less, with 4 or 5 persons to each one, in its five divisions of San Mateo, Zebolleta, or Cañon, Chusca, Hozo, Chelli with its thousand men of arms; that their possessions consist of 500 tame horses; 600 mares with their corresponding stallions and young; about 700 black ewes; 40 cows along with their bulls and calves, all looked after with the greatest care and diligence for their increase." Another writer of the same year, 1795, states, ". . . they work their wool with more delicacy and taste than the Spaniards. Men as well as women go decently clothed, and their captains are rarely without silver jewelry."[2] In 1799 an officer of the Spanish Royal Engineers wrote, "The Navahos have manufacture of serge blankets and other coarse cloths which more than suffice for the consumption of their own people, and they go to the Province of New Mexico with their surplus and there exchange their goods for such others as they have not, or for implements they need." In 1812 Pedro Pino, who went as a delegate to the Spanish Parliament, wrote of the Navaho: "Their woolen fabrics are the most valuable in our province and in Sonora and Chihuahua as well."[3]

The picture evoked by these quotations indicates that within the thirty-two years between 1780 and 1812, Navaho weavers, through their imagination, versatility, and increasing skill, had gained widespread recognition throughout the Southwest.

A later picture is given by Charles Bent in 1846:

> Navaho war and hunting parties might be found anywhere from the Coconini Plateau in Arizona to the buffalo plains of West Texas. They rarely ventured as far north as the Arkansas [river] and so were little seen at Bent's Fort. They did, however, go often to Taos to trade, many of their woven blankets finding their way into the Bent, St. Vrain and Company store, and ending up finally at the Fort as trade goods valued by the Plains Indians.[4]

THE PROCESS

***The Wool.*** The sheep that have been raised by the Navaho over a long period of time are small, are resistant to the desert heat and sudden changes of

[1] Charles Avery Amsden, *Navaho Weaving*, p. 130.
[2] *Ibid.*, p. 131.
[3] *Ibid.*, p. 133.
[4] Frank McNitt, *The Indian Traders*, p. 35.

weather, can survive cold winters, and can exist on a minimum of food and water. Consequently, the fleeces of these sheep are light, and comparatively free of grease. The staple of the wool is long and wavy, and is particularly suited to Navaho methods of hand spinning.

Under the adverse conditions of raising sheep on most of the reservation, where flocks range over great distances in order to find enough to eat, heavier breeds, such as the Rambouillet, have difficulty in surviving. The crimpy wool from the Rambouillet is very difficult to spin by hand, and when it is used it is apt to produce lumpy strands. The traders and the commercial wool buyers, however, have wanted heavier meat-producing animals and heavier fleeces. The difference in the character of the wool between the old-type sheep and new heavier breeds has been one of the major factors in the controversy over introducing the newer strains, for it is the Navaho women who usually control the sheep, and they want the old-type wool. While only 10 percent of the wool crop is used for spinning and 40 percent for sale to wool buyers, that 10 percent, by the time it has been transformed into fine rugs, brings a greater return than the wool that is sold.

Nevertheless, so much Rambouillet blood had been introduced into the Navaho flocks by 1936, in order to satisfy the demands of both traders and commercial wool buyers, that the type of wool needed by the weavers was in danger of extinction. The Rambouillet sheep, though heavier and better meat and fleece producers, did not thrive on reservation pasture. To meet this situation, the Department of Agriculture commenced a project at Fort Wingate, known as the Navajo Sheep Breeding Laboratory, under the direction of J. O. Grandstaff. Its purpose was to develop a breed of sheep that would have the conformation of the Rambouillet and the wool quality of the old Navaho sheep, as well as the ability to subsist on reservation pasture. During the more than twenty-five years since its inception, this Laboratory has succeeded in fulfilling its purpose. Not only has the mutton conformation been achieved while retaining the subsistence hardiness of the old sheep, but also the quality of the wool has actually been improved.

The Bureau of Indian Affairs was working with the Laboratory during part of this time, endeavoring to interest the Navaho in improving their flocks. To accomplish this improvement it was necessary to keep the new sheep separated from other stock, and this proved to be very difficult. Whenever Navaho breeders would agree to this program, they were loaned three bucks of the new breed. The Bureau, however, did not have the personnel, nor did the Laboratory, to do the much needed field work. The Navaho themselves as yet have not shown sufficient interest in the project. Perhaps it followed too closely on the sheep reduction program for them to realize what the benefits really were. The Sheep Breeding Laboratory still exists, furnishing bucks to a few Navaho and Zuñi breeders, and at the present time there are some one thousand head of this new breed. What seems to be needed is an effort on the part of the Navaho themselves to profit from this long experiment. The Laboratory furnishes wool from these sheep to the Arts and Crafts Guild, already washed and carded and ready to be hand spun, but many of the weavers think it is too costly. It is hoped that where there are a number of weavers in a given area they will unite to improve the weaving wool for their own looms. The benefit they would receive would repay them many times over, but changes such as this take time to bring about.

Many goats are also raised by the Navaho, who like the meat to eat just as well as mutton, and goat hair (mohair) is also used in weaving. More difficult to spin, it nevertheless produces fine yarn, and rugs made of mohair bring a premium.

In Santa Fe, in 1860, there were a number of German merchants who imported from Germany the fine vegetal-dyed Saxony yarn with intent to sell it to the weavers of the Rio Grande Valley. It is believed by some authorities that some of this wool reached Navaho weavers, possibly while they were in exile at Fort Sumner. Having little or no wool of their own production, they may well have used this soft three-ply yarn if it became available to them at that time.

There are in existence, mostly in museums, a number of extremely handsome and rare blankets woven by Navaho women between the years 1860-1880, all made of this fine Saxony yarn. Following this period, American-made Germantown yarn made its appearance at some of the trading posts on the reservation. Heavier than the Saxony yarn, four-ply instead of

three, it was used to some extent during the decade that followed, and, with this yarn, cotton warp was first used. The cost of the Germantown yarn was a deterrent to the weavers, who, in general, preferred to continue spinning their own wool, and, in addition, the traders objected to the use of the cotton warp, which is neither strong nor elastic.

*Shearing.* In early times, sheep were shorn with the use of any piece of thin metal that could be honed to as sharp an edge as possible on a stone. But when metal shears were first brought to the trading posts, the Navaho were quick to use them. The shorn wool is sorted carefully, the weaver separating the longest hairs to use as warp, removing the shortest to be sold as wool, and saving the remainder for spinning weft threads. Burrs and other matter sticking to the wool are carefully removed.

*Washing.* Usually only greasy wool is washed. Using the pounded roots of the yucca plant for soap (still preferred by most weavers), and making a rich lather with it in a pan or a tub, the weaver pours the mixture over the wool as it lies on a slanting board or rock, repeating until all the dirt, sand, and grease have been removed. The wool is then spread out in the sun to dry, and finally stored in sacks ready for use.

*Carding.* In early times cards consisted of burrs

*Wool is still carded by hand.*

held in place by strips of leather mounted on small boards with handles at one side. These were replaced when metal cards of American manufacture were procurable at the trading posts. When a weaver is ready to card her wool, she first loosens it by hand, then combs it between carding tools until the hairs lie all in one direction. Carded wool emerges in the form of soft pads called "rovings," ready to be twisted into continuous strands. If a weaver wants to produce good gray color, she mixes wool from black sheep with that of white as she cards the wool. This method makes the finest gray used in many rugs, particularly those from the Two Gray Hills area.

***Spinning.*** The Navaho spindle differs from that of the Pueblo spinners, and its method of use also differs greatly. The spindle consists of a round stick about twenty-five to thirty inches long, pointed at both ends. The whorl is a flat disk, four or five inches in diameter, with a hole in the center into which the stick fits. The whorl, which acts as a balance, is securely fastened to the stick about five inches from the butt end.

The spinner first attaches a roving to the upper end of the spindle, and, with the butt end resting on the ground, she starts a roving onto the spindle with a spinning motion of the stick. Then, resting the upper part of the spindle on her thigh, she rolls the spindle with the palm of her right hand in a drawing motion toward her body. With the free end of the roving held in her left hand out from the top of the stick, she stretches the wool as it slips off the top of the twirling spindle (as shown in the picture of Old Lady Long Salt). The skill lies in the steady motion of the spindle as she twirls it with her right hand, while at the same time she uses just the right amount of pull to stretch the twisting strands. As a given length of roving is twisted and stretched into yarn, the spinner winds it onto the spindle just above the whorl, where it is stored until she has a sufficient amount to wind off into a ball. Each successive spinning makes the yarn finer and stronger. All Navaho yarn is spun at least twice until it is smooth and fine, and all yarn is one ply with the exception of the two-ply cords made for the selvages, so characteristic of Navaho weaving.

The quality of the wool, even more than the skill of the spinner, determines the character of the yarn. Coarse, short-fibered wool cannot be spun into smooth fine yarn, but wool from the old-type Navaho sheep almost spins itself. This is why the weavers objected to the introduction of the Rambouillet sheep.

Since the American occupation of the Southwest, traders and others have tried to introduce the spinning wheel, but the Navaho women have always rejected it, probably because of the lack of room in the hogans, and the nonportability of the spinning wheel. Perhaps now that so many Navaho move less frequently and have sufficient space in their modern houses, they might be more interested in this less laborious method of hand spinning.

***Dyeing.*** Using a wide variety of native plants, the Navaho produce dyes of many colors and shades. The wool from black sheep is never a true black, as it tends toward a brownish tinge. Good black dye is made from a mixture of twigs and leaves of sumac boiled four or five hours and then added to a mixture of powdered native yellow ochre and an equal amount of piñon gum; both mixtures are stirred together over a fire until a black liquid is formed which dries to a fine black powder. The tannic acid of the sumac acts as a mordant to produce a rich, permanent black.

Indigo, on the other hand, was imported in lumps by the early traders and was used extensively until the end of the 1890's. The indigo, tied in a cloth, was suspended in a large jar of urine which acted as a mordant. Occasionally, some of this dye is still made. The wool was placed in the jar and left until the desired depth of color was obtained. The mordant used with most native plants is an impure alum found in limited quantities in certain regions on the reservation, while some plants require moss or lichen as a mordant.

Aniline dyes, perfected in 1856–1857, came onto the market from the first factory in 1864, and were in general use by 1870. They reached the Navaho traders about 1880 when Mr. B. F. Hyatt, trader at Fort Defiance, taught the weavers how to use them. C. N. Cotton, originally a partner of Lorenzo Hubbell, succeeded in obtaining dyes packaged ready for use, including a mordant, and these, under the trade name of Diamond Dyes, were soon available at most trading posts, and were used to dye native hand-spun wool.

***The Loom.*** The structure of the loom is both simple and practical. It consists of two parts: the weaving frame and the stationary upright poles and cross beams which hold the weaving frame while in use. Looms are made of native wood, poles of a desired

*At age 94, Old Lady Long Salt of Navaho Mountain was still spinning her wool.*

height being set into the ground with top and bottom cross beams. Usually the top cross beam is held in place by natural crotches at the top of the upright poles, while the lower beam is securely tied at the bottom of the loom frame. These cross beams support the weaving frame after the warp has been strung to it.

When a weaver has determined the size of the rug or blanket she will make, she first prepares the warp. A warping frame is made of four long poles, of which the two longer ones are cut some twelve to eighteen inches longer than the rug to be woven. On top of these poles she places two shorter cross pieces, sometimes broomsticks, tying each corner very securely, taking care that all sides are parallel and the measurements accurate. She then raises this frame a little above the ground on low supports, just high enough so that a wound ball of warp thread will pass beneath the cross sticks. After tying one end of the warp thread at the top (usually the upper left-hand corner), she passes the ball over and under the lower stick, and then up over and down under the top stick, thereby creating the cross of the threads, continuing until the sufficient number of threads have been wound. The winding of the warp is most carefully done, the weaver making certain that the threads are straight, that the tension is even, and that no threads are twisted or crossed. She ties the last thread at the diagonal of the first tie.

Next she adds the end cords. These consist of two- or three-ply twisted strands of weft threads which have been measured twice the width of the rug. These are twined with each other as the edging is woven in and out of alternate warp threads, the weaver keeping the spacing and tension even for both the top and bottom edges. Next comes the preserving of the cross formed at the center of the warp by the over and under winding of the warp threads. The weaver places a small reed (the length of the rug width) on each side of the cross, tying the reeds to hold this cross in place. The four poles of the warping frame are then removed, leaving a mass of warp threads, in which the cross is preserved by the reeds, and the top and bottom end cords hold the ends of the warp in place. The end cords are then tied to the weaving-frame cross bars by weft threads which wind around the bars holding the edges securely to it. The creation of the firm top and bottom edges is one of the perfections of the Navaho technique. When the rug is finished it is removed from the loom simply by untying the edges from the loom cross bars. Sometimes this winding thread, which holds the edges in place on the loom, is placed between every two warp threads, sometimes every three or six, depending on the size and whether the rug will be woven of coarse or fine material. The bottom cross piece of the weaving frame is then tied to the bottom cross beam of the loom, and the top piece is laced to the top cross beam by a rope, using large loops by which the tension of the weaving frame can be adjusted. Again great care is used to see that all cross pieces are parallel.

The next procedure is the tying in of the heddles to form one or more of the sheds through which the weft is passed. The heddles are tied to every other warp thread for a plain weave, or to combinations of threads for any other weaving pattern the weaver chooses. Sometimes several heddles are used, as in the diamond-twill or herringbone weaves.

Yarn for the side edge cords is then tied to the lower beam, and loosely tied to the top beam. If the warp threads are light in color, the side edge cords are usually made of weft color threads, made in the same way as the top and bottom edge cords. The loom is now set for the weaver to commence weaving the rug. Everything about the loom has been made of simple native material and is completely functional.

***Weaving.*** The simple tools used in weaving number only two—the comb and the batten—though every weaver will have several sizes of each. The comb is made of a hard wood into which tines have been cut, like a fork, perhaps three inches in length, with a handle carved out at the opposite end. The comb is used first to beat down the weft as it is passed through the shed. The batten, also made of hard wood, is a slightly curved piece about thirty inches long and three inches wide, though smaller sizes are also used. One shed is formed by the shed rod, the long upper stick just above the heddle; the other shed is formed by the heddles. The batten is inserted in the shed and then turned edgewise to make the opening wide enough for the insertion of the weft to be passed through. A true shuttle has never been used by the Navaho, for they insert the weft with their fingers, except when weaving plain long stripes; then a small stick is used,

*Daisy Tauglechee produces many of the finest rugs.*

*The weaver is dyeing wool in a solution made from a native plant called Navaho Tea.*

*This woman is preparing to dye wool with the yellow root of the Holly-grape.*

*Because this rug is too wide to weave an entire row from one sitting position, the weaver commences several rows before moving over to complete them. Here the heddles are tied to every other warp thread.*

*These three pictures show clearly the process of weaving: the shed stick at the top of the warp, then three heddle sticks, then the battens, one turned on edge to spread the warp.* ABOVE, *a stick is being used as a shuttle;* AT LEFT, *the usual hand method is seen.* ABOVE, *a diamond twill;* ON THE RIGHT, *a herringbone weave. The picture on the right also shows the top and side edge cords.*

around which weft thread has been wound. As so many of the designs require only a few inches of color at a time, the nimble fingers of the weavers seem adequate. As weaving is done in a sitting position, many weavers do not complete a whole line at a time when this would require moving, but weave several inches from one position before moving over to complete the line. After the weft has been passed through the shed, first the comb is used to press down the weft, then the batten; it is used also to press down over a longer area. The degree of firmness struck with both comb and batten determines the tightness of the weave.

The variety of weaves attained by the Navaho weavers is great: from the plain weave to the tapestry weave, the diagonal and the diamond twills, the rare two-faced weave which has a different design on each side, and the wedge weave, unique to Navaho weavers. Added to the variety of weaves are the variations of color and pattern, giving the weaver an extensive choice.

Most of the designs are carried in the weaver's mind. She does not use a diagram or drawing or counting of threads. The exceptions are some of the very intricate patterns of tapestry sand-painting rugs, or some of the classical designs—then the weaver makes a sketch in the sand. This carrying of a design mentally is a remarkable feat, for every weaver has many interruptions, and sometimes may be away from the loom for days at a time; yet when she returns to her loom she knows the exact place in her design where she had stopped and what is to come next.

***Knitting.*** The Navaho also practice knitting, though interestingly enough it is usually the men who knit, making leggings or footless stockings. Originally sticks of hard wood were used for needles; later, wire or the ribs of old umbrellas served well. Regular knitting needles were of course carried by the traders when the demand for them became manifest.

As many as four or five needles are used at a time. The knitters create a raised rim at the top of the stocking with a purl stitch, giving a firm edge for longer wear. A knitted or plaited band is added at the bottom to pass under the foot to keep the stocking from working upward.

### THE BLANKETS

From the beginning of Navaho weaving, blankets and mantas were made for clothing. Beyond personal needs, as the chroniclers have told us, surplus blankets were made for trade. The great period, known as the classic period, was from approximately 1840 to the end of the nineteenth century. During the earliest part of this period, possibly even before, Spanish traders brought a fabric known as bayeta cloth to trade to the Indians. This was imported from England to Spain, thence to New Mexico, and, while it was called by the Spanish name, it was in reality English Manchester cloth. Red color predominated, a special shade of red which took the fancy of the Navaho weavers, who unraveled it, and, after careful scrutiny to test its strength and evenness, sometimes respun it, and then wove it into the intricate patterns of these early blankets. Many of the finest examples of Navaho weaving contain the beautiful bayeta, merged into the textiles along with the native hand-spun wool. Many serapes and blankets of this period were so firmly woven that they were waterproof. They were in great demand and were highly prized.

From about 1890 until the early years of this century, Navaho weaving deteriorated. The weavers commenced making coarser fabrics, largely for sale to the tourist trade as floor rugs. To a considerable extent the traders were responsible for this change. With the making of rugs rather than blankets, borders were introduced with patterns of very different character from the fine, vigorous designs of the classic period. Mr. J. B. Moore, of Crystal, seems to have been the first to suggest the idea of borders to the weavers of his area. This suggestion carried across the mountains to Two Gray Hills, where it was developed and has been used extensively ever since. In the early 1880's, Mr. C. N. Cotton left Ganado, where he had been a partner of Lorenzo Hubbell, to establish a wholesale business in Gallup, for he was intent on developing an eastern market for both blankets and rugs. With the coming of the railroad in 1882–1883, the outlook for such a business increased. As the Fred Harvey Company of the Santa Fe Railroad built its Harvey Houses along the length of the line, it not only used Navaho rugs in the buildings, but developed shops where the travelers might purchase rugs and other Indian-made handicrafts. Rugmaking grew to be a great business, the entire output being sold to the American public.

*The skilled hands and the fine yarn of Daisie Tauglechee.*

In 1920 Miss Mary C. Wheelwright of Boston, who at that time owned a shop carrying Indian-made articles for sale, had a talk with trader L. H. (Cozy) McSparron at Chinle. One of the questions Miss Wheelright asked was did he know if the Navaho weavers still knew how to use their old vegetable dyes? Both Miss Wheelwright and Mr. McSparron deplored the trend of commercial dyes and loss of the fine old designs. McSparron agreed to see what he could do to persuade the weavers of his region to return to the old dyes. After some experimenting, some of the weavers produced borderless simple designs with the wool dyed by their old native methods. Mr. McSparron was able to sell these at a higher price than those made of commercial dyes, and to sell them as fast as the weavers could produce them.[5] This was the beginning of another great change in the production of rugs, for other traders soon followed McSparron's lead, and, today, thousands of these beautiful rugs are on the market.

The Two Gray Hills region, however, has continued the border-patterned rugs which are woven with natural white, gray, brown, and black wool. The gray is a mixture produced by carding natural white with some black. The black is dyed to produce a true color, while a rich brown is obtained with dye made from a native walnut.

Occasionally, very large rugs have been made on special order, measuring twenty or more feet wide by nearly forty feet long. Special looms had to be built to accommodate such size, but they were, or are, built to the traditional specifications. Rugs of extremely fine texture have appeared in recent years from the Two Gray Hills area. One weaver, Daisie Tauglechee, spins strands so fine that her woven fabric counts 110 weft threads to the inch. Others are now following her lead, but, so far, these are still bordered rugs and of the undyed wool, except for the black and the brown.

Throughout the nearly 175 years that the Navaho women have been weavers, they have produced an extraordinary variety of products; moving quickly from the first simple striped blankets to the superb classic period, through a time of decadence, until in very recent years a new surge of fine quality has appeared. The variety of design seems endless in its use of geometric shapes, the spacing of line and color, and the harmony of the whole, for there are never two exactly alike.

The variety of weaving is also great, for, following the old original clothes that were woven, there are shoulder blankets, ponchos, serapes, saddle blankets of both single and double weave, rugs, Yei blankets (sand-painting blankets), saddle girths, sashes, garters, hair-cords, stockings, and leggings. Weaving is unquestionably the great craft of the Navaho. The finest examples are to be found in leading museums of the world, as well as in many private collections. The new building of the Arts and Crafts Guild at Window Rock, with its contents of weaving, silver jewelry, and other crafts, is evidence of the vigorous production of the craftsmen of today. If the yearly volume of Navaho handicrafts which are sold by the many traders and shops all over the Southwest and elsewhere were added together, the aggregate would be impressive.

*The Silversmiths*

The art of silversmithing commenced in earnest among the Navaho soon after the return from Fort Sumner, though there may well have been earlier efforts. That a few individuals knew the craft of blacksmithing before the exile is recorded in Richard Van Valkenburgh's *Brief History of the Navaho People.* He attributes this knowledge to Captain Henry L. Dodge, the first civil agent to live in the Navaho country, though there may well have been previous knowledge of the craft. Captain Dodge was a veteran of the Washington Expedition of 1849, and he both understood and sympathized with the Navaho. Following his appointment in 1853, Captain Dodge built a house on the eastern slope of the Chuska Mountains not far from Sheep Springs, commencing his work with a Congressional appropriation of $5,000. One of the first things he did was to bring a blacksmith, George Carter, an ex-soldier, to teach smithing to the Navaho in his area. He also brought a Mexican silversmith. But Captain Dodge's career was of short duration, for he was killed from ambush by the Chiricahua Apaches south of Zuñi in 1856 while on a hunting trip with a group of Navaho chiefs.

It is probable that the Navaho had worked in metal

[5] Amsden, *Navaho Weaving*, p. 224.

*The five major weaves of the Navaho.* TOP, *wedge weave, unique to the Navaho;* LEFT CENTER, *herringbone saddle blanket;* CENTER, *two-faced small blanket with a different pattern on each side;* RIGHT CENTER, *diamond-twill saddle blanket (there are several different kinds of twills);* BOTTOM, *a classic period blanket woven with bayeta.*

even in the eighteenth century, and that inability to obtain silver may well have been the reason why they did not work in this medium at an earlier date. While there are a number of references to Navaho people wearing silver jewelry prior to the exile, it was doubtless obtained through trade or capture from the Spaniards, Mexicans, or even Plains Indian tribes, such as the Utes or Kiowa, who sometimes came in contact with the Navaho. Many of the designs later adopted by the Navaho were of Spanish origin, such as the so-called Squash Blossom, which in reality is the pomegranate blossom long used by the Spanish in Europe, fashioned of brass or silver for buttons, and of iron for ornaments on spurs.

One of the early Navaho to ply the blacksmith's trade was Atsidi Sani, who became known as a maker of bridle bits and knife blades. In his authoritative book, *The Navaho and Pueblo Silversmiths,* John Adair tells of Atsidi Sani's learning the silversmith's art from Nakai Tsosi, a Mexican craftsman who lived near Mount Taylor (Tsoodził).

As there seems to be no record of any silver work by the Navaho prior to the exile to Fort Sumner, it must have been after their return in 1868 that practice of the art commenced. That it spread rapidly is evident from all the early records of the period between 1870 and 1880, for by the time that Dr. Washington Matthews was stationed at Fort Wingate at the latter date, there were a good many proficient craftsmen. Dr. Matthews employed two Navaho silversmiths, whom he established near his residence where he might observe them at their work, and he left for posterity a detailed account of the art as practiced by these two men. Some fifty years later, Father Berard Haile also left a similar

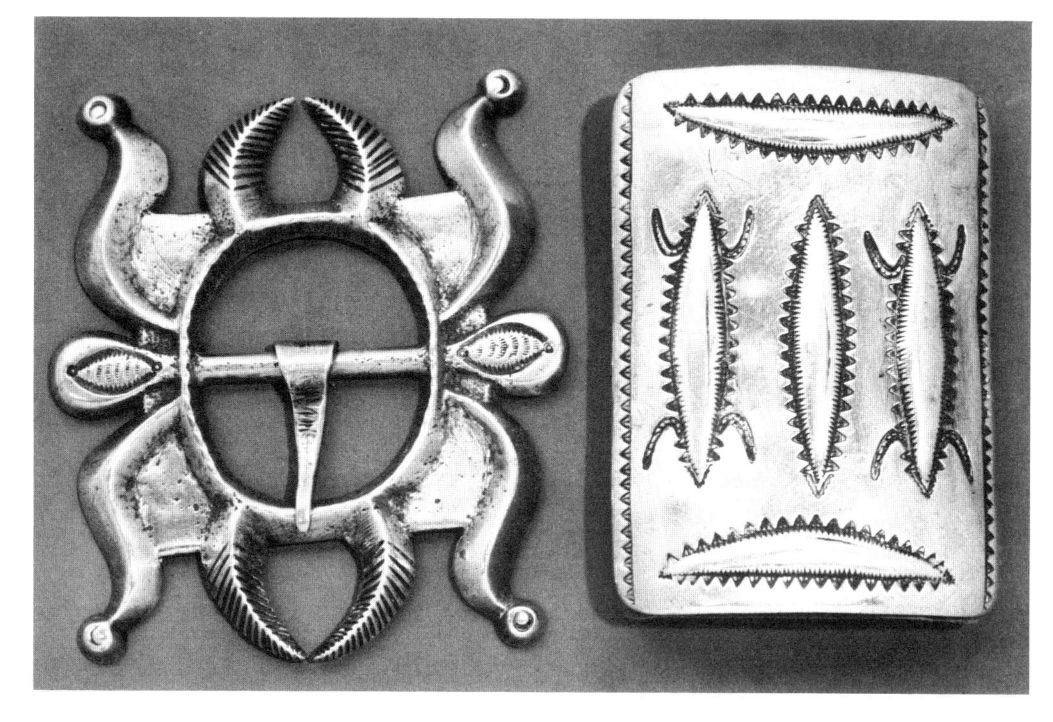

record of his findings over a wider area, for he had been making a study of silversmiths as well as of many other subjects during his long years on the reservation.

The fine work of the early Navaho smiths was produced with the simplest of equipment, and though during the following decades new tools were added to the smith's work bench, the technique is basically the same.

THE METHOD

***The Forge.*** The forge was a square structure of stones and adobe mud, built to a convenient height with the rear slightly elevated. Air tubes were made of two pieces of wood, grooved and fitted together and lined both inside and out with adobe. The smith sat crosslegged on the floor of his hogan or wherever he had his forge. In later years benches or chairs were used to give a more comfortable sitting position for long hours of work.

***The Bellows.*** The bellows was made of sheepskin in the form of a sack about eighteen inches in diameter, held distended by three or more hoops of willow twigs. One end of the bellows was firmly secured to a nozzle and fitted into one of the tubes leading to the forge. The other end was closed by tacking the sheepskin to a round disk of wood containing a leather valve in the center. The bellows had two handles of different lengths; the longer projected downward, resting on the ground, the upper worked the bellows. As the number of silversmiths increased, traders stocked commercial bellows in their posts.

***The Anvil.*** The very earliest anvils were simply hard stones. Later, pieces of iron, such as parts of plows or wagons, were used. After the coming of the railroad, pieces of rails were used and still are by many smiths. An anvil was fastened to the top of a large log cut to the right height for comfortable work.

***The Crucible.*** The early crucibles for melting silver were made of clay, and baked hard in a fire. They were about three or four inches in diameter and had an outward-curved rim and one or more spouts. These melting pots were not very durable and were replaced by commercial crucibles when they became available. Some smiths have found that cup-shaped pieces of prehistoric pottery from a ruin served the purpose and were more durable than any other container.

***The Mold.*** Some ingot molds are made for cast-

*A silversmith at work in 1934. In the winter Navaho men often wear headbands made of fur—there is no top.*

ing bars of silver, which will be worked into bracelets or other ornaments. Molds for making casts are incised in a soft stone, preferably pieces of volcanic tuff, a very light pumicelike stone which is found in several places on the reservation.

The incised pieces of tuff for casts are cut to approximately the right size and shape and the surface is perfectly smoothed. A cover piece is then fitted to each mold, making as tight a fit as possible. Grooves are cut at one end of the incised piece to permit the entry of the molten silver, while two or more grooves are cut for air passages.

All molds for casting are greased with mutton tallow. Molds for beads are cut into iron or hard wood, smooth surfaced, so that the silver coin or sheet can be pounded into the depression, making a rounded half of a bead. Later two of these are soldered together to make the spherical bead.

*The Smelting Fuel.* Charcoal has always been used for smelting fuel. It is prepared during the summer months from large fires of piñon or juniper branches. After the flames have died down and only glowing embers remain, the coals are smothered with earth and allowed to cool, forming the charcoal.

*The Blowpipe.* Originally the blowpipe was hammered out of a piece of brass or copper wire, bent into a tube with a curved, tapering end. It was used in soldering with a lamp or wick of twisted cotton soaked in tallow. The modern blowtorch is a highly prized tool used today by most smiths. Some ingenious individuals have fashioned torches from cans by fastening a spout on one side and forming an opening on the opposite side into which a rubber tube is fastened. Blowing through the tube produces enough pressure to blow the flame out the spout.

*The Solder.* Silver solder is used with borax as flux to make it flow smoothly.

*The Materials.* Some of the very early smiths worked in copper and brass, making rings and bracelets. The first silver to be used was American coin silver, melted and fashioned to the desire of the craftsman. When the United States government put a stop to the use of coins for this purpose, some time in the 1880's, the traders soon procured Mexican pesos in their place. The Navaho smiths preferred the peso silver, for it had less alloy and was somewhat softer. As the traders began to buy jewelry to sell, they provided silver in one-ounce slugs in a quality approximately that of the coins.

*The Stones.* Turquoise first was used by the Navaho

*Taking a cast medallion from the mold.*

*In recent years Navaho women have also become silversmiths.*

in the 1880 period. The traders procured stones from mines near Santa Fe, and later from mines in Colorado and in Utah. The traders supplied stones that sometimes were already cut, and sometimes were in chunks that had to be shaped and polished. Early stones were set in deep bezels, with the edges coming slightly over the top of the stones, holding them securely in place. As craftsmen acquired greater skills they were able to set stones in a lower setting. Other kinds of stones also were used—malachite, garnets, cannel coal.

***Cleaning.*** The Navaho liked their silver well polished. Silver used to be cleaned with native alum, and then polished with buckskin, but today it is cleaned by being dipped in a diluted solution of nitric acid, then put in a bowl of water and brushed with a wire brush. It is buffed either by hand or with a buffing pad attached to a grindstone, with the pad well covered with jeweler's rouge.

The skill of the Navaho craftsman lies in his ability and judgment in all phases of his work—sprinkling a little borax on the silver as it melts, to reduce the melting point; heating the silver to just the right degree of even moltenness; pouring the molten silver quickly and evenly, to avoid the formation of a slight crust causing brittleness and, later, cracks. There is great skill in using the hammer correctly, striking blows with the edge of the hammer and producing blows of even strength. Coins are hammered by hand, the smith singing as he works, obtaining a rhythm of song and stroke. The most beautiful of the silver ornaments are the hand-hammered pieces. The smith must learn to use his dies correctly, placing them exactly and striking them with just the right amount of force. These techniques of course require much time to achieve.

The Navaho made jewelry primarily for his own adornment and that of his family. It was not long, however, until there was a ready market and a growing demand for his products. Just prior to 1900, the Fred Harvey Company realized this potential market and began to place orders with traders who had silversmiths in their regions. Soon came a demand for lighter (in weight) pieces at lower cost, so that silversmiths were producing two types of jewelry, the old heavy pieces for their fellow Navaho, and light-weight cheaper jewelry to sell to the white man.

The traders began to stock better tools for the smiths—dividers, files of many sizes and degrees of fineness, metal worker's saws, and gasoline blow torches. The smith usually made his dies, with which he stamped designs on bracelets and other pieces, from all sorts of worn tools, old railroad spikes, old cold chisels, bolts, and other pieces of scrap. The Nav-

aho never wastes anything; he always seems to find a way to put worn-out scraps to use. And seldom does he ever make two pieces alike; there is always a difference, giving his work that unmistakable quality of hand work, and the uniqueness of Navaho design.

The Navaho learns the techniques and methods of his craft from watching another smith, usually a relative. The apprentice pays for his instruction by helping his teacher as soon as he is able. In rare cases when a man is learning from a nonrelative, he pays for his apprenticeship in sheep, or cash, or some other material way. The Navaho, when he does not have the money to buy the tools he needs, shows great ingenuity and resourcefulness in his ability to fashion such tools from old material.

ARTICLES OF JEWELRY

***Conchas.*** The round or oval disks called *conchas* are made for ornamenting belts and bridles. Sometimes these are very simple, sometimes ornate with design or turquoise studding.

***Buckles.*** Silver buckles are made for belts and bridles; other metals are used for girth buckles.

***Bridles.*** Headstalls are mounted with silver bars with various degrees of ornamentation. *Conchas* are used sometimes at joints with larger bars, sometimes on a pendant from the cross piece over the head of the horse.

***Ketohs.*** Long ago the Navaho adopted the use of a leather wrist guard as a protection from the snap of the bow string. Later, silver ornaments were added to the guard, or *ketoh*. Some are of hammered silver, many are beautiful casts, and some are set with turquoise. Today they are worn as ornaments and are always worn on dress occasions. As these have never been made for commercial use, they are the finest of the silversmith's art.

***Bracelets.*** The Navaho silversmiths make many types of bracelets: Some are bands of silver one or two, even three, inches wide with simple or ornate decoration. Some are heavy and mounted with turquoise; some are narrow with or without stones; some are narrow with stamped designs. There are also cast bracelets with open design, with or without turquoise.

***Necklaces.*** Necklaces are made of hollow beads of many sizes and shapes, constructed in two pieces and soldered together. Sometimes the so-called squash blossom ornaments are strung at intervals between the beads. Many necklaces have pendant Najah, a design similar to the Arabian hand of Fatima (probably brought to New Mexico by the Spanish). Some early Najah had two little chiselled hands at the ends to ward off the evil eye; this is doubtless a Navaho adaptation. One also finds small circles with inset turquoise at the ends. Sometimes this nearly circular design is double. There are many other types of necklaces—strings of turquoise, of shell ground into very fine beads, and of coral.

*Soldering silver squash blossoms for a necklace.*

*Carving a mold for a bracelet.*

***Rings.*** The earliest rings were plain silver bands; soon some were made with simple incised designs. The use of turquoise with silver appeared in the early 1880's. Some cast rings were made. Most rings now have insets, usually turquoise, but also malachite and garnets or cannel coal, and occasionally polished petrified wood.

***Pins.*** There are pins of many shapes and designs, both with and without turquoise.

***Earrings.*** Both Navaho men and women have worn earrings since the early days. Before the advent of turquoise on the reservation, Navaho men wore silver earrings of several types: round circular loops on which dangling silver beads had been strung; flat slightly decorated rings; and pendants, narrow and cone shaped with spreading flowerlike petals at the ends. Since turquoise became abundant, about 1900, the silver earrings for men have all but disappeared. Instead the men wear large pieces of turquoise in several forms—some edged with silver, others plain

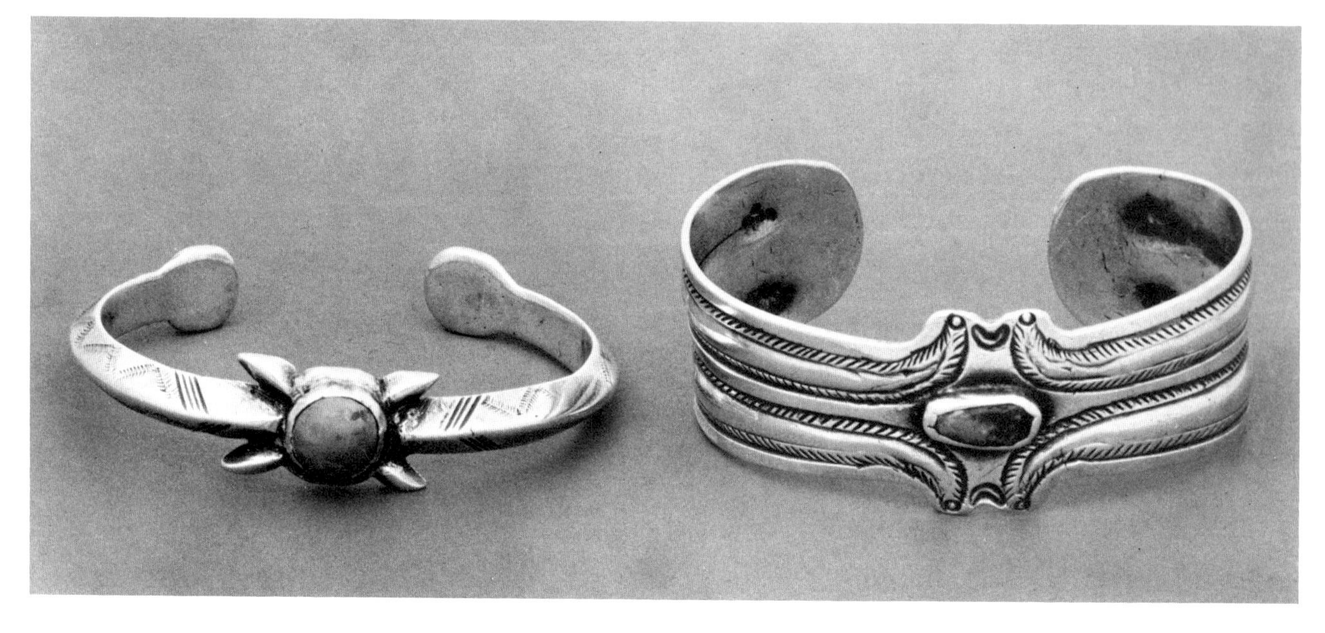

with holes drilled in one end for the insertion of string, which in turn is passed through the pierced ear. Women too, have long worn earrings, usually turquoise beads strung in loops two to four inches long with the addition of a few bits of red shell at the bottom of the loop. These are worn on string passed through pierced ears.

Sometime in the 1920's, the Fred Harvey Company introduced the screwtype fasteners, urging silversmiths to produce women's earrings to be sold through the Company to the non-Indian market. In recent times Navaho women also wear the screwtype earrings with both silver and turquoise ornamentation of great variety.

***Buttons.*** The variety of buttons is great, hammered silver as well as cast. There are many sizes and many shapes, such as buttons with small turquoise insets, plain silver disks, and some with incised designs. Coins which have loops soldered on one side are often used. Buttons are used as ornaments on collars, cuffs, blouses, leggings, moccasins, pouches, and narrow leather straps.

***Unusual Pieces.*** *The Mother-in-Law Bells* are made from twenty-five-cent pieces, hammered into thin bell shapes. The coins are pounded between a round-headed bar into a corresponding receptacle of hard wood or iron. Small clappers are fastened to the inside, and the bell is then fastened to the end of a short string of beads. These are made for older women who wear them on their belts to notify their sons-in-law of their approach.

*The Powder Horn* was a gracefully designed receptacle to hold a charge of powder. It had a handle on one end, the whole object being shaped like an elongated letter S. A small chain was fastened to the center for attachment to a belt. When bullets were available, powder horns were no longer made, and, as many were probably melted down to make other articles, they soon became very rare.

*Tobacco Canteens* were beautiful small containers, seldom made any more. Only a few are in existence, mostly in museums and private collections.

A variety of other pieces are being made today for sale to the non-Indian public, such as spoons, silver boxes, and a number of other articles.

When the Arts and Crafts Guild was founded in 1940, under the direction of René D'Harnoncourt of the National Indian Arts and Crafts Board, John Adair was appointed as the Guild's first manager. Mr. Adair's extensive knowledge of Indian crafts made him the ideal person to commence this Guild. Ambrose Roanhorse, one of the most skilled Navaho

*Ned Hatathli, first Navaho manager of the Arts and Craft Guild.*

craftsmen, was his assistant, and together they made a solid beginning for the Guild, setting the highest standard for materials and workmanship. Following World War II, when the Guild was re-activated, other managers took Mr. Adair's place, one of whom trained a young Navaho, Ned Hatathli, to follow in his footsteps.

In 1951 the Guild was made a Tribal enterprise, with Ned appointed as the first Navaho manager. The Guild grew rapidly under Ned's management as more and more craftsmen brought in their products for sale. Housed at first in the old log building at the Fair Grounds, the Guild has recently moved to a beautiful new building erected by the tribe on the highway approaching Window Rock. Here fine facilities display great quantities of rugs, jewelry, and other items coming from the skilled hands of the Navaho. The total output from the looms and forges on the reservation is great, for in addition to all the many traders both on and off the reservation who handle

*Ambrose Roanhorse with his class at Fort Wingate school.*

these products in quantity, the total amount of sales by the Guild alone came to a quarter of a million dollars in 1963.

Ned Hatathli went on to become a member of the Tribal Council in 1955, serving in this capacity until 1960, when he was made director of Tribal resources, the position he now so ably holds.

Away from the reservation, there is a quantity of imitation Navaho jewelry on the market. Any purchaser will do well to go to reliable shops or directly to the Guild at Window Rock, where all items bear the seal of the Arts and Crafts Guild, and all are of unique Navaho design.

Ambrose Roanhorse, whose superb work as a master silversmith has won him many awards, including a decoration from France, is now teaching at the Vocational School at Fort Wingate, near Gallup, where boys and girls are given the opportunity to learn not only all the Navaho Crafts, but also other occupations, such as carpentry, shoe making, leather work, and dressmaking—trades that will equip these students for their future lives.

*The Potters*

Following the Spanish reoccupation of New Mexico, 1692, some Pueblo Indians fled into Old Navaholand. During recent archaeological excavations in this area, evidence came to light of the close proximity of these Pueblo groups to those of the Navaho. In the ensuing century, pottery fragments from Navaho sites indicate, there was a definite Pueblo influence, such as sherds decorated with red, black, and occasionally white designs which had been fired to the high temperature used by the Pueblo people.

Later came utilitarian pieces, some of good size, with thin walls made of crumbly clay with sand for temper. Shaped with the use of corncob scrapers, many pieces had exceptionally beautiful form. These storage jars had pointed bottoms, being held upright by the use of basket rings or by being set in depressions in the floor. Water bottles were also made of pottery in early times. Shaped somewhat like a pitcher without a spout, such a pot had a loop, a finger handle, near the narrow neck to facilitate pouring. A horsehair rope could also have been inserted in the loop for easier carrying. These bottles were flattened on one side for ease in carrying, and some had designs. Legend tells of water bottles being made of the four sacred colors—white, blue, yellow, and black—and used in ceremonies to carry water gathered from the four sacred mountains. These water bottles are very rare now, for they were replaced by other types of containers as soon as they became available. Bowls of various shapes and sizes, spoons and dippers and dolls, many with finely executed designs, were the products of years gone by.

Today, only cooking jars, a few bowls, and drums are made, and there seem to be but few potters left. These jars, somewhat similar in shape, rounded on the bottom with a slight flare at the top, and some with scalloped edges, are all that can be found of recent manufacture. These jars or pots are made for cooking or for preparing dyes for wool, while some are made specially for remedial and ceremonial use. A few of the latter are used as drums with pieces of sheepskin or goatskin stretched over the tops. A new pot is always preferred for a drum and once it has been used for this purpose it must never be used for cooking.

In some areas firing of the pottery is accomplished by the potter's first digging a pit and then building in it a large fire of piñon wood. When this has burned down, the coals are raked to one side, the pots put in, usually upside down, covered with the hot coals, and, then left for from four to seven hours. In other areas, pots are placed on flat stones, then covered with enough juniper (preferably) to insure the fire's burning for six hours without replenishing. A few areas have used Spanish-type outdoor ovens. After a good fire has burned down, the pots are placed in the oven and left for twelve hours. Pottery making among the Navaho has never approached the superlative quality of that of the Pueblo craftsmen. Because the Navaho often moved from place to place, pottery was replaced by more durable containers as they became available, with the exception of the jar-type vessel, which is used also for ceremonial purposes.

*One of the few remaining potters.*

Following many inquiries in numerous regions, I finally heard of one potter still at work in the Shonto area. With an English-speaking interpreter, Betsy and I set off to find her. After looking at my pictures and learning what I wanted to do, she asked us to return in two days, when she would be ready. As there are a number of taboos connected with pottery making, I was not at all sure what I would be able to accomplish. For instance, no one must watch the gathering and grinding of potsherds (from ancient pueblo sites) which the Navaho potters use for temper to mix with their clay. This had been prepared and mixed with the clay before we arrived, but our potter did leave the metate (grinding stone) and a few sherds for us to see. May Adson, our potter, was sitting beneath a shelter as we drove up, and greeted us with the usual Navaho courtesy. We watched her make four pots, employing much the same technique as that of the Pueblo potters, using a waterworn stone for smoothing the inside and a piece of corncob as a scraper on the outside.

Before May fired these pots, we had lunch. We had

also been watching one of May's daughters prepare the meal, which consisted of roasted corn on the cob, boiled mutton, coffee, and fry bread, a dough patted into a round flat cake and fried in deep fat. We produced some fresh fruit from our larder, and as we ate we listened to much Navaho conversation. Finally after a few silent moments our interpreter turned to me and said, "You two look kind of old, but you sure got good teeth!"

Lunch over and everything put away, our hostess built up the fire and placed the pots near it. This was in no sense true firing. She turned the pots occasionally to heat them evenly all around; these were baked rather than fired. Two of the pots we purchased to bring home, but we were sure that, because we had witnessed as well as photographed their making, the others would never be used, and would be destroyed after we had gone. However, we had had a nice day and had witnessed at least part of the Navaho pottery-making process.

When we were packed and ready to leave, May shyly said to us, "We have a new baby in the hogan." I had noticed another woman going in and out of the hogan several times during the day, but she did not join us nor speak to us. We were taken into the hogan where we found a tiny baby less than twenty-four hours old. It was on a small cradleboard, sound asleep. Soon, the father would make a permanent cradleboard for the addition to the family. We parted good friends and went on our way, for we had located a basketmaker not too many miles away, whom we were to visit the following day.

*The Basketmakers*

While the art of basketmaking is a minor craft among the Navaho, it is practiced with great skill by the few women who still make baskets. From the time of the return from exile, three types of baskets have been made, but in recent years two of these are no longer found, the water bottle and the carrying basket. The water bottle had a long neck and a round base, measuring from twelve to sixteen inches in diameter. It was coated both inside and out with pitch or resin to make it watertight. The carrying basket was a wicker, loosely woven basket with an unfinished edge, used for gathering yucca or cactus fruit or other edible plants. As other types of containers came into the trading posts, these two types quickly disappeared.

From 1868 to the early years of the twentieth century, shallow baskets were made for ceremonial use, for utilitarian purposes, and for holding small objects. Archaeological evidence indicates that graves did contain baskets, though in recent times they are never buried with the dead.

During the past fifty years or more, baskets have been made exclusively for ceremonial use. These are shallow, perhaps three to four inches deep and twelve to sixteen or eighteen inches wide. The material used is chiefly sumac, sewn with split strips of sumac leaves. A bone awl is used to insert the yucca binding strips. The sumac twigs, or small branches, are scraped clean and sorted as to size; pieces to be dyed are laid to one side, others will remain the natural color. The same dyes as are used for wool are prepared for the dying of the sumac. Usually only red, indigo, and black are used, occasionally yellow.

DYES

*Red* is made from the roots of juniper and mountain mahogany boiled together, and then ground, with alder bark added to the mixture.

*Navaho basketmakers are dwindling in number.*

*Blue* is made from the same indigo dye as is prepared for dying wool. Also used is a native blue, which is made from a blueish clay and ochre mixed together, pulverized, and moistened with water.

*Black* is obtained from coal added to boiling sumac leaves, or from a sulphurous rock, slightly roasted with piñon gum or resin. Added to boiling sumac, this gives a rich, lustrous black.

The basketmaker begins by winding a sumac twig around a small stick called the "bottom of the basket." In order to assure that it will be pliable, all material is soaked before being used. Sewing is done counter-clockwise, with the exception of one rare ceremonial basket which is made clockwise and which must be completed in one day. So deft and strong is the sewing that a basket will require only a few minutes of soaking to make it watertight.

#### DESIGNS

Designs are limited to geometrical shapes and tiered block patterns, sometimes used in a single row, sometimes in double rows with the second inverted. Sometimes a single open unit is used, sometimes bands with no geometric forms are used. Always there is the "trail" or "path of exit," the "spirit path," a narrow strip where the design does not quite meet, for the Navaho believe that to complete the circle would imprison the spirit of the maker. This is also true of some Pueblo potters, for a similar trail will be found on much decorated pottery. When a basket is nearly complete, the rim is finished in a herringbone, or false braid, technique. The final end of the rim is always directly above the spirit path. In ceremonies where a basket is full, the medicine man knows where the spirit path is by finding the end of the rim, and the basket is placed so that the spirit path always faces the east.

Baskets have numerous ritual uses: as drums by turning them upside down and beating on them with small drumsticks; as containers of ritual parapherna-lia, such as prayer sticks, medicine bags, and fetishes; as containers for use in ritual baths; and as food containers in certain ceremonials, for example, corn-meal porridge in wedding ceremonies, this use having given them the name of wedding baskets. Occasionally baskets are used as portions of masks in certain nine-night ceremonials and in certain minor rituals in the hogan.

Strict taboos exist in connection with basketmaking, as with all the other crafts. While a woman is making a basket she must not be touched by anyone. No one may step over the materials being used to make a basket, otherwise the material will break. Should a man make a basket, he will become impotent. Blood must never touch a ceremonial basket. Should this taboo be broken, harm will come not only to the maker, but also to the singer who used it. In silver-smithing, too, the craftsman must not make certain pieces of jewelry while his wife is pregnant or some disaster will occur.

Other crafts pursued by the Navaho are many kinds of leather work, both decorated and plain—saddles, shoes and moccasins, pouches, straps and belts, hobbles, quirts and ropes. In early times the Navaho became good tanners, for they made shields, quivers for their arrows, and leather caplike helmets. To whatever craft the Navaho turns his talents, he will execute it with skill and dexterity.

### *The Painters*

Aside from the ancient rock paintings, the art of painting is a comparatively new venture for the Navaho. However, as early as 1901, Dr. Kenneth Chapman, while working at Chaco Canyon, discovered a Navaho boy making drawings with colored pencils. But it was not until much later that any serious work was done. In 1932 the Santa Fe Indian School commenced a class in painting under the direction of Dorothy Dunn, in which several of the now-famous Navaho painters had their start. In that same year three Navaho boys made a series of murals in the school dining room under the supervision of Olive Rush, the well-known Santa Fe artist, who had great interest in developing the painters' art among both Navaho and Pueblo Indian students.

Such famous painters as Gerald Nailor, who painted the murals in the Tribal Council room at Window Rock, and murals in the Department of Interior in Washington, had his start in Miss Dunn's class. And there were many more: Andrew Tsihnajinnie, Ha-So-De, Quincy Tahoma, and Harrison Begay, whose portrait is here. Later artists were Beatien Yazz, Wade Hadley, and others. Today many more young Navaho are doing excellent work at the new Institute of American Indian Art in Santa Fe.

One interesting aspect of painting by Indian artists,

*Harrison Begay—one of many fine artists.*

not only Navaho but many others as well, is their method of work, which is instinctively Oriental. Pictures are painted from knowledge and inner vision rather than from a direct approach. Instead of an easel, a Navaho painter works on a flat surface. There is always an extraordinary sense of design, a skilled sure draftsmanship, and the Indian's subtle use of color. Museums all over this country and in Europe own examples of Indian painting, many of them by Navaho artists. One can truly say that all American Indians have artistic potential. The amazing amount of talent that is coming to light at the new Institute, now in its third year, is ample proof of this latent ability.

# PART III

# THE COMING WAY

# TRIBAL GOVERNMENT

PRIOR TO THE OCCUPATION of the Southwest by the United States, the Navaho existed as bands of people, usually either clans or groups of clans. They were united only by language and by tribal culture; they had no political entity or sense of responsibility to these isolated groups. There were chiefs, or headmen, chosen by each band, but there seemed no need for any further government. Certainly the Spanish government of the seventeenth to the early nineteenth centuries did not realize the independence of these Navaho bands, nor did the Mexican government during its twenty-five–year duration. Nor was it fully comprehended by our government until the time of the exile to Fort Sumner, if then. It was during these years that General Carleton tried to establish a simple form of self-government, but the old order of family and clans seemed unchangeable and any other form was incomprehensible to the Navaho.

There were many notable characters among the chiefs of the early 1800's, most of them destined to become prisoners of war—exiles to Fort Sumner. The names of twenty-eight Navaho leaders appear on the Treaty of 1868, signed by General Sherman for the United States, and the Navaho leaders for their respective bands, including such personages as Barboncito, Manuelito, Narbona, Ganado Muchos, and others.

After the return to the reservation in 1868 and the establishment of the Navaho Agency at Fort Defiance, the old order continued. The first civil agent to the Navaho, Captain Henry L. Dodge, utilized the Navaho leaders to assist him in maintaining law and order. As time went on and more agents appeared on the scene, the federal government found it necessary to be more autocratic. By 1901, the Bureau of Indian Affairs divided the Navaho country into six districts (including the Hopi), with an agency in each. This system of smaller areas of jurisdiction greatly facilitated the work of each agency, but it did nothing to bring the Tribe together as a whole. Communication was still difficult, and in many areas, travel was possible only by foot or on horseback. Each political change in Washington brought a new commissioner of Indian affairs, who usually had new ideas and adopted changes in policy that must have been bewildering to the Navaho.

It was the discovery of oil on the reservation in 1921 that brought to focus the need for tribal government for all the people. This discovery, located in the San Juan District near Shiprock, immediately brought about discussion as to whether oil leases were to be executed by this District Agency, or by the Tribe as a whole. The Treaty of 1868 required the consent of at least three fourths of all adult male Navaho from all parts of the reservation to determine the cession of any region. Therefore, the secretary of the interior ruled that these oil leases should be for the benefit of the whole Tribe, and authorized the Indian commissioner to sign oil and gas leases in their behalf. At the same time the establishment of the first Council was designated, to be selected from this large percentage of the male population. The next year a "Business Council" was formed to act for the Council—those chosen were Chee Dodge, long a powerful leader in the tribe, Charlie Mitchell, and Dugal Chee Bekiss.

In 1923 the first Navaho Tribal Council was elected, holding its first meeting on July 7 of that year. The chairman was chosen from outside the Council membership, with one of the delegates being selected as vice-chairman. Thus Chee Dodge became the first chairman of the Navaho Council, serving from 1923 to 1928. Meetings of the Council were called by the Navaho agent of the Bureau of Indian Affairs, rather than by the commissioner, and could be held only in his presence, the meetings to be held for a period of two days annually. This first Council, bringing together one delegate and one alternate from each of the six districts, was soon found to be inadequate and was followed with revisions; a second Council met in the same year, and again in 1927 and 1928, when voting rights for women were added. Only the outline of Navaho government as it has progressed since its inception is given here, interesting as it is, for a full account would entail many pages.[1]

In 1927, Superintendent John Hunter, of the Leupp Agency in the southwestern part of the reservation, developed a local community organization called a Chapter. Meetings of this group made it possible to bring together the people of the region where representatives from the Bureau of Indian Affairs could discuss the Bureau's efforts for the betterment of agricultural conditions, the improvement of livestock, and the necessity for schools. This Chapter plan proved most beneficial as the people gathered to discuss their problems among themselves as well as with the officials. The idea spread quickly to the other districts, bringing better understanding between the Navaho People and the Bureau.

In 1931, the Council was increased to its present number of seventy-four delegates, these to be elected by the people of the districts in accordance with the population of each district. Those first ballots were pieces of ribbon of different colors, each candidate having a selected color. Leadership beyond the local level was still difficult for the people to comprehend, and by 1936 there were criticisms that the Council membership was not representative of the Tribe. It was the issuance of grazing controls that brought home to each locality the fact that the Council members rather than the local headmen were making the decisions.

Voting registration was adopted in 1938, and ballots with pictures of the candidates on them were used, as there were still many voters who could not read or write. There have been attempts to draw up a constitution for the Navaho Tribe, but as yet no satisfactory document has been achieved.

Many changes have come about from the late 1930's to the present, as the Navaho People as a whole have been learning the ways of government. During the formative years from 1923 to 1938, there were four chairmen of the Tribal Council: Chee Dodge, Desha Chischillige, Thomas Dodge (Chee's son), and Henry Taliman. The growth of the tribal government continued and the time for the Council meetings was increased from four days a year to one hundred, being divided into four sessions. Compensation for both Council and officers has likewise increased as the demands on the individuals' time have lengthened

[1] For a fuller account see "Origin and Development of Navajo Tribal Government," *Navajo Yearbook*, pp. 371–429.

*The Navaho make use of ceremonial gatherings to discuss either local or tribal problems. When we arrived at the Squaw Dance on the mountain above Red Rock in 1934, we found this Chapter meeting in progress.*

*Since the erection of the new Tribal Council building at Window Rock, all Council meetings are held here. On the walls are beautiful murals depicting the life and history of the People, painted by the Navaho artist Gerald Nailor.*

*With Sam Ahkeah as chairman, Manuelito Begay rises to discuss problems in his Crownpoint area.*

*Navaho women casting their votes at the poll.*

until today the positions of officers are full-time responsibilities. With the election of Jacob Morgan in 1938, progress was accelerated, and though there have been controversies, the work of the Council has held a steady forward movement. Chee Dodge was again elected chairman in 1942 (with Sam Ahkeah as vice-chairman), holding this office until his death near the end of his term. An Advisory Committee has been formed to take care of business when the Council is not in session, and enlargements and improvements in the structure of the Navaho government have been adopted as their need became apparent.

The administration of Sam Ahkeah, 1946–1955, marked a point of great change and development for the Navaho People, for his sound and wise judgment brought many beneficial acts of legislation. He continued the organization of the Tribal government, bringing capable Navaho into positions previously held by non-Indian personnel wherever they met the approval of the Navaho Agency and the commissioner of Indian affiairs, for it has been the policy of the Bureau to help the Navaho develop their own government as individuals came forward with the ability to serve.

Sam Ahkeah commenced a survey of the mineral resources of the reservation which eventually led to

*Chairman Sam Ahkeah, 1946–1954.*

the discovery of uranium ore and new oil fields. It was Sam, who, with his staff and attorney, located tribal funds accumulated from oil revenue between the years 1922 and 1946, deposited in the National Treasury to the credit of the Tribe. Realizing that the interest from this money was not coming into the tribal treasury, Sam went to Washington, where he discovered the sum of $200,000 in accumulated interest. With these funds available, Sam planned other new developments for the benefit of his people.

To the outsider it seems that on the whole the wealth that has come to the Tribe has been wisely used, yet in the 1963 election campaign, unproved accusations of misappropriation of funds were made. After sixteen years of comparatively smooth progress, controversy has arisen in the Council following the election of Raymond Nakai, the present chairman. As a reaction to his eagerness to bring quick reforms with his administration, differences of opinion have emerged between the older councilmen and the newly elected younger members, resulting in a division in the Council. Good may come from this, for the People as a whole have become aware that some tribal matters have come to a stand-still, bringing about the realization of the importance of each individual vote. These troubled times may well lead to a more truly democratic government, even, possibly, a two-party system. The situation at Window Rock today may be compared to a time when a President of the United States is elected by one party while the majority of the Congress belongs to the other. Doubtless the 1966 election will resolve many of these differences.

Aside from this monetary situation, the record of progress and development of the tribal government since its beginning in 1923 is most remarkable, for the People, who formerly had no governing body other than the leadership of chosen headmen, now are welding themselves into tribal unity showing great advancement in consideration for the Tribe as a whole.

### *Recent Tribal Leaders*

#### SAM AHKEAH

Sam Ahkeah, who became chairman of the Tribal Council in 1946 following the death of Chee Dodge, was born March 8, 1896. He grew up in the Shiprock area, going to school at Fort Lewis, near Durango, Colorado. As a young man he worked at Mesa Verde National Park, later moving to Santa Fe for a position at the Laboratory of Anthropology. During his years away from the reservation, Sam was quietly learning the ways of the white man—methods of business, the way government was conducted—and in many ways preparing himself for his role as leader of the Tribe.

In 1954 I went to Window Rock at the time of the tribal election when Sam was defeated by Paul Jones. While Sam had served nearly two full terms, he had been elected for the office only once. But many of the Navaho felt that he was running for a third term, and voted therefore against him. The day after the returns were all in, I asked Sam if I might make his portrait. I wanted to do this in the Council room, at the chairman's desk, so we went over to the Council building. While I was setting up my equipment, I said to him, "Sam, you have done a wonderful work for your people since you have been chairman." He was silent for a few minutes, then he said, "Well, I think I have waked them up to what they can do for themselves." This eloquent remark summed up his eight years of hard work in the fewest possible words, for indeed he had aroused his people to their own potentials in this changing world.

I once heard such a nice story about Sam. During one of those years when he was making frequent trips to Washington on Tribal business, his son was in training at an Army base nearby. Meeting his father at the station, the soldier son urged that they take a sightseeing tour of the capital city. They went up the Washington Monument, traveled to Mount Vernon, saw the Smithsonian Institution, and visited the Library of Congress, spending a busy day. The next morning when they got into a taxi, Sam gave the driver a new destination. As they drove up to the steps of the Nation's Capitol, Sam's son said, "Gee, Dad, I can't take you in here," little realizing that his father was a well-known personality at the Capitol, as Sam, of course, had been present for Senate hearings on Navaho tribal affairs during his years as chairman of the Tribal Council. Sam answered, "I know, son, but I can take you." So they went in to see the senator from New Mexico, Dennis Chavez. It was Senator Chavez who later obtained tickets for Sam to hear President Roosevelt's last address to the Congress of the United States.

*Chairman Paul Jones, 1954–1962.*

### PAUL JONES

Following Sam Ahkeah's two terms in office, eight years of steady growth, Paul Jones was elected chairman in 1954, serving for two terms. Continuing Sam's program, he also commenced many new projects, including the building of community centers, the development of the tribal park system with the establishment of the first tribal park at Monument Valley, while other parks are still pending.

Large sums of money were coming into the treasury from the uranium mines and the new oil fields. Much of this income has been soundly invested, the rest providing many new benefits for the Tribe, such as greater water development, new and better roads, new hospital facilities in collaboration with the Public Health Service, the establishment of the Education Scholarship Fund, the Tribal Enterprises, and the ten-day work program whereby every Navaho in need of work is guaranteed ten days of work a month –an impressive list of accomplishments.

Paul Jones, whose administration continued this great progress of the Navaho People, was born October 20, 1895, near Tohatchi, New Mexico. Following his elementary schooling he served for three years as an interpreter for a missionary doctor of the Christian Reformed Church. He entered high school in Englewood, New Jersey, and obtained his college education at Calvin College in Grand Rapids, Michigan. During World War I he served one year overseas in France, Germany, and Italy. As he had been gassed during the war, he was physically unable to continue his education after his release from the Armed Services.

Following two years on the reservation, during which time he recovered his health, he entered a business college in Grand Rapids, but before completing his course he took a business position in Chicago. In July, 1933, he returned to the reservation with his family to commence work for the Bureau of Indian Affairs, which he served in several capacities, including interpreter and liaison representative at Window Rock. Later he was district supervisor at Piñon, Arizona. He was elected chairman of the Tribal Council in 1955.

*Maurice McCabe, treasurer of the Tribe in 1954.*

Mr. Jones is a member of the New Mexico Commission on Indian Affairs (appointed by the governor), the Arizona Commission on Indian Affairs (appointed by the governor), the Arizona Civil Rights Advisory Commission, the Governors' Interstate Indian Council (composed of members from seventeen states), the National Boy Scouts of America, and the President's Committee on Job Opportunities, and served as a delegate to the Fourth Inter-Indian Conference in Guatemala. He has been awarded the Silver Beaver Medal by the Boy Scouts of America, and the Practical Humanitarian Award by the Federation of Women's Clubs, Washington, D. C.

### J. MAURICE MC CABE

J. Maurice McCabe, at present director of business administration, is a thoroughly dedicated person in the service of his people. He has a great sense of order, one of the basic qualities of Navaho life, now transformed into modern methods. At the beginning of Sam Ahkeah's second term, in 1951, Maurice was appointed treasurer of the Tribe, a position he held for many years. As the tribal government developed he became more and more absorbed in tribal work. Though he won a scholarship award, given by the John Hay Whitney Foundation for further study in business administration, he declined the scholarship due to the need for his work for the tribe.

Maurice McCabe was born at Tohatchi, New Mexico, on October 18, 1923. He is a direct descendant of Barboncito, one of the great early leaders of the Navaho People and one of the signers of the Treaty of 1868. Maurice received his elementary education at the Tohatchi School, at the Presbyterian Mission School in Ganado, Arizona, and at the Christian Reformed Mission School in Rehoboth, New Mexico. He graduated from the Methodist Mission High School at Farmington, New Mexico, in 1941. Shortly thereafter it was discovered that he had tuberculosis and he was sent to a hospital in Phoenix, Arizona. Though bedridden for about two years, he studied business and business law, and when he was able to be up and about he entered a business college, finding employment as a bookkeeper on the side. In 1946 he was promoted to the position of office manager for a chemical company where he was employed.

Following the election of Paul Jones as chairman of the Tribal Council, Maurice was asked to continue his services as treasurer, and to assist Mr. Jones in the complex affairs of the Tribe after the development of uranium and of oil and gas, as the need for expert business administration had become increasingly demanding. In 1957, by resolution of the Council, Maurice's position was changed to executive secretary, with special designation of duties, and a specific directive to propose a reorganization of the tribal staff, which was needed to meet the increasing executive demands of tribal business. To accomplish this, he sought the advice of a Remington Rand expert to establish the most efficient record system for the ever growing files of the Tribe. When an emergency stock feeding program was needed at a time of extreme drought, the United States government sent large quantities of surplus grain to aid small Navaho stockmen who were threatened with high losses. To keep exact account of this transaction, Maurice procured IBM machines to complete these records in accordance with the government regulations. The reorganization of the tribal offices has now been accomplished and, under Maurice's direction, continues in a most efficient manner.

Maurice has been active in other fields concerning the Navaho People. He was a leader in the establishment of the Education Scholarship Fund, the development of Boy and Girl Scout organizations on the reservation, and most recently the establishment of the Navaho Youth Camp, now under construction, which will benefit not only Navaho boys and girls, but also children from other camp organizations.

While I was at Window Rock in 1954 I wanted to include Maurice's portrait in my tribal government series. Finding that one of his great prides was the Council Room with its fine murals by Gerald Nailor, I suggested the Council Room for a background. A year later, when I was there again, I found that Maurice had been to New York and had visited the United Nations. As a result of what he observed there, each Council member now has a nice desk with a name plate.

Like his famous ancestor, Maurice is indeed a leader with vision and the ability to bring that vision into reality as he continues his service to the Navaho People.

### ANNIE WAUNEKA

Large in stature, vigorous and strong in both mind and body, Annie Wauneka is a dynamic personality. Daughter of Chee Dodge, the first chairman of the Tribal Council, Annie was born April 10, 1910, and received her early education in the reservation schools. In 1951 Annie was elected to the Tribal Council, the first woman to serve in this capacity, and she was shortly named chairman of the Committee on Health and Welfare, a position she still holds.

On July 1, 1955, the United States Public Health Service assumed the work of the Department of Health of the Bureau of Indian Affairs, and soon thereafter expanded both its facilities and services. Annie Wauneka's role became, almost immediately, one of interpretation and communication. Her achievement has been tremendous in helping to carry out this increased program for Navaho health, as she has fulfilled her part with great determination. One of the first problems to be undertaken was in the field of tuberculosis, for there were many Navaho afflicted with this disease. Contagion and germs were two totally unknown concepts, and had no meaning to most of the Navaho People; therefore, Annie undertook an educational program, instructing her people in antisepsis, and attempting to win not only their cooperation in combating the further spread of the disease, but also their faith in the white doctors.

The Public Health Service arranged with a number of sanatariums in several of the Western states to include Navaho patients. Annie persuaded many ill Navaho to accept this offer, and during those early years of this program she visited every hospital, and talked to all the Navaho patients, urging them to learn how to prevent contagion, to accept the rest cure, and to listen to the instructions of the doctors. A number of these patients, finding themselves in totally strange surroundings and among people they did not know nor to whom they could talk, became homesick and ran away. Annie brought them back, teaching them to understand the necessity for their convalescence. She helped produce a motion picture illustrating the cure and prevention of tuberculosis, and acted as interpreter for the doctors and as a liaison personage whenever one was needed. All this was an heroic task which Annie pursued vigorously, using her own knowledge and persuasive powers to win these many Navaho into acceptance of their condition and the necessity for its cure.

Annie Wauneka has received numerous awards for her achievement: From the Arizona Public Health Association, an award as "outstanding worker in public health"; the Josephine B. Hughes Memorial Award, given by the Arizona Press Women's Association; the Indian Achievement Award, and others. To

*Annie Wauneka in 1954.*

crown them all, she was one of three women named by President John F. Kennedy on July 4, 1963, to receive the Medal of Freedom. This was presented to her by President Johnson in the White House ceremony on December 6 of that year.

As Annie herself has said, "Now I must work harder than ever," and indeed that is what she is doing. With tuberculosis now well under control and diminishing, other problems are occupying her attention, such as dysentery among Navaho children, and Alcoholics Anonymous groups. She has her own radio program, broadcasting regularly in the Navaho language from a station in Gallup, reaching the many Navaho who today have radios.

One of those rare personalities having complete singleness of purpose and the determination and strength to carry it through, Annie Wauneka has won the respect and admiration not only of her own people, but also of the many doctors, officials, and all with whom she has come in contact during her years of service on the Tribal Council.

*Wearing the Freedom Medal, 1964.*

*Health and Education*

Shortly after the return of the Navaho to their own country following the exile to Fort Sumner, the first effort to offer an educational program resulted in complete failure. A small day school was opened at Fort Defiance in 1870 with a very few children attending. They stayed to satisfy their curiosity and to receive some clothes which were donated, then they vanished, and all efforts to bring them back proved fruitless. In 1883 the first boarding school was started at Fort Defiance, fraught with problems of insufficient funds and staff. This school also lasted but a short time. Then the government turned to the missionaries, who were appearing on the scene wanting to be of some benefit to the Indians, and suggested that they establish both missions and schools. There were four early missions, each adding a school as soon as possible. The first was a Methodist school at Hogback, near Farmington, which soon was moved into that town. The second was the mission at St. Michael's, established by the Franciscan Order in 1898, with a school opened in 1902 by the Sisters of the Blessed Sacrament. The Presbyterian Mission at Ganado, Arizona, was the third, established in 1901, with a school opening the following year and a hospital ten years later; and the fourth was a mission founded by the Christian Reformed Church at Rehoboth, near Gallup, also in 1898, with a school opening shortly thereafter. Other denominations followed in several areas of the reservation, some with special emphasis on medical aid.

These early endeavors were beset by many trials and tribulations caused by the natural suspicion of both Navaho children and their parents, many of whom did not wish their children away from home where they were needed to tend the sheep. The policy of forcing the children to go to school was an unfortunate one. It is a matter of record that there were even instances of physical brutality due, doubtless, to lack of understanding of Navaho ways, and to the sheer frustration on the part of some staff members finding themselves so isolated, so helpless in performing their tasks under conditions of hardship and remoteness.

Slowly the Indian Service progressed with many varied endeavors; new schools were built, and some children did attend. But the policy of forcing education on the Navaho provided many stumbling blocks. For a long time children were forbidden to speak Navaho, or to wear Navaho clothes, and everything

*A classroom at the Crystal school with Navaho teacher Ester Henderson.*

*Children at the Red Rock Day School.*

possible was done to try to superimpose our culture onto that of the Navaho. Some children from twelve to sixteen were sent away to schools in California and to a number of schools in the East, with the intent of merging them into our society, but this was too much to expect in a few short years. More than 95 percent of these children came home where they found themselves to be misfits, for they were unaccustomed to reservation life.

With the coming of the New Deal a different policy was adopted, due in part to the road improvement program, to develop new day schools, bringing children to school by bus, just as in any county in the country. One other practical development of the new policy was the establishment of a number of trailer schools located in areas where small children could reach them from their homes, giving these youngsters the advantage of early education. These were big steps in the progress of education and soon many well-trained teachers with modern methods in teaching and with better understanding of the Navaho undertook the new teaching jobs. Some teachers created a desire on the part of the children to learn; some teachers even conducted adult education classes in the evenings, with people coming from miles away to attend. Navaho teachers were also coming into the picture, bringing, of course, the best possible relationship between children and teacher. But there were still many more children of school age than there were facilities for them. The Indian Service Educational System continued to grow and improve, until there came a day when many children were clamoring to go to school. Yet there were also those who were, and some who still are, shy and diffident, and there are backward areas, as in every state in the Union, but there are many hundreds who are absorbing their school work like little dry sponges, and who go on into fields of more advanced learning.

The slow process in education is paralleled in medicine. For many years it was unthinkable for a Navaho to turn to a white medicine man. But slowly progress has been made in such fields as the eye disease trachoma and other special lines. Since World War II young non-Indian doctors have come to work at some of the hospitals and health centers, finding themselves filled with enthusiasm for their People and the work to be done, and for the first time bringing a new psychological approach to their endeavor. And though there have been superstitions to overcome, as well as the difficulties of winning trust, the doctors have forged ahead with progress in many ways. It has been here that Annie Wauneka has done so much in the field of interpretation, one of the doctor's major problems. They did not know it was forbidden for a younger person (who was acting as interpreter) to ask his elders many personal questions. The doctors were puzzled by the vagueness of many answers. But Annie had a solution: there must be a glossary prepared of medical terms in English and Navaho, with a simplified explanation as well. Annie was insistent that this be done. A young Navaho woman was selected to go to the premedical school at Cornell University, where she spent two years preparing this glossary. It has been highly successful and of great benefit to the many doctors working on the reservation.

Through help from the Education Scholarship Fund, the first Navaho doctor is now practicing at the Kayenta hospital, and there are many Navaho nurses (both registered and practical), dentists, and technicians, with many more in training. As this number grows, there will come a day when the Navaho will care for their own.

Since the Public Health Service took over the Indian Bureau medical program, there have been many developments, such as new hospitals, new health centers, and new health stations with accompanying services. Also there have been several privately sponsored clinics, such as that conducted by Cornell University at Many Farms, where I found a Navaho technician at work with the Cornell doctors. While there is yet much to be accomplished, as everywhere else, the acceleration of medical care for the Navaho during the past ten or fifteen years has accomplished a great deal for their benefit.

### EDUCATION SCHOLARSHIP FUND

One of the most worthwhile acts of the Tribal Council has been the establishment of the Education Scholarship Fund for higher learning. In 1953 a sum of five million dollars (later increased to ten million), accrued from oil, gas, and uranium earnings, was set aside for the special purpose of giving aid to honor students who were selected for these grants. One of these students is Herbert Blatchford, who graduated

*The clinic at Many Farms conducted by Cornell University*

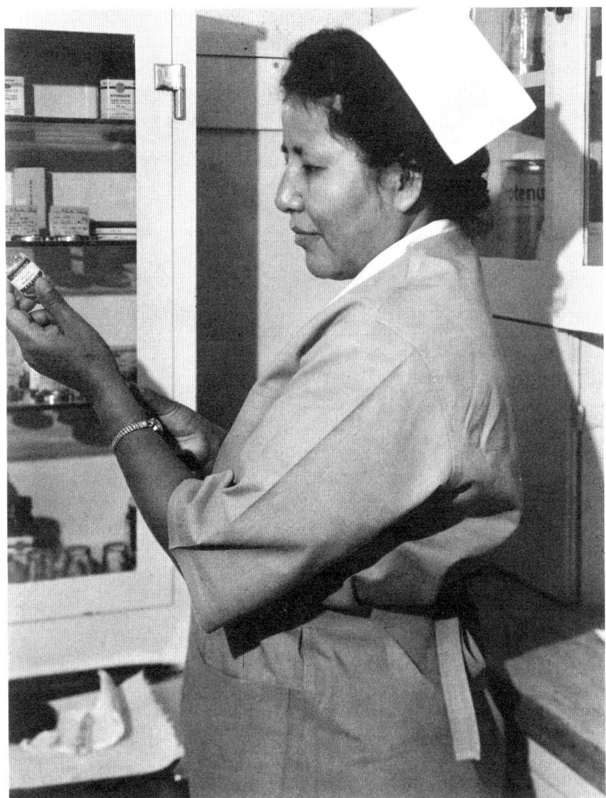

*A Navaho trained nurse at the Fort Defiance Hospital.*

from the University of New Mexico in 1956, where he majored in education. His first work was for the McKinley County Public Schools as an attendance counselor, working out of Gallup, New Mexico. In these schools Navaho children were being accepted with the regular school body, and it was Herbert's duty to check on any absentees. I went with Herbert into the area surrounding Gallup, to see just what his field work was in this capacity. At one hogan there was an eleven-year-old girl who had been absent from school for several weeks. Herbert went directly to the child, not to the parents. We entered the hogan where Herbert began talking to the child. Seeing that she was very shy, I thought my presence there might be disturbing to her, so I went outside to wait. Soon I heard voices in conversation as Herbert was getting answers to his questions. Then there was a long quiet talk from Herbert as he told the child how important it was for her to continue her studies, and what her schooling could mean to her in later life. When they joined me outside, the child was smiling happily, seemingly pleased indeed with all she had learned from her counselor.

As we drove off, I asked Herbert what had been the difficulty. His answer, "Oh, teacher trouble." Then I learned that there were a number of teachers in the Gallup schools who were new to New Mexico and unfamiliar with Indian children. In the course of our conversation it emerged that Herbert had organized an evening class for these teachers to help them understand the Navaho children. This he did on his own initiative, showing unusual judgment in finding a practical method to solve some of the problems of these children. Realizing that he needed some knowledge of law, Herbert returned to the University for a year's work in this field.

In 1963 the members of the Tribal Council, together with representatives of McKinley County and the city of Gallup, appointed Herbert as manager of the Gallup Indian Community Center. There had long been a great need in Gallup for a place where visiting Indians could get a night's lodging for a nominal cost, a place where they could meet and have some form of recreation, a place with a cafeteria and other facilities. This building, erected in 1952 through the Navaho-Hopi Rehabilitation Act, was operated for a number of years by the Unitarian Service Committee. Now the Board of Directors of the Community Center has taken it over, and is operating it with the united help of the Navaho Tribe and the city of Gallup.

In addition to all the work as manager of the Center, Herbert is acting also as a counselor to any young Navaho who are seeking employment off the reservation, or are having difficulties in their present jobs. He sponsors good educational programs and supervises various recreational activities for all ages as they come to use the facilities of the Center. At present he is also working with the New Mexico Commission on Alcoholism and Alcoholics Anonymous groups in the big effort to overcome the drinking problem in this area. He gave me encouraging figures—that more than 50 percent of those treated are remaining in good health. It is to be hoped that this progress will continue, for alcoholism has been a serious problem ever since the Indian prohibition law was repealed.

In whatever future work Herbert undertakes, his clear thinking and scholarly mind will stand him in good stead. He has an extraordinary command of the English language, and may someday prove to be an able writer.

Another honor student to be educated through the Scholarship Fund is Nancy Rose Benally Evans. Nancy Rose was born in Shiprock in 1938. She went first to the grade school in Shiprock, then to the Indian School in Albuquerque, and then to the University of New Mexico, where she majored in biology. As Nancy Rose thought it silly to waste whole summers while getting her education, she enrolled in the summer schools at the University of New Mexico and also the University of Colorado. The result, of course, was that she graduated in three years instead of four. She went right on to get her master's degree, which she received in 1961 at the age of twenty-three. Continuing her studies, she completed two years toward her doctorate, acting also as a research assistant to the head of the Department of Physiology at the University, as well as doing part-time research at an Albuquerque hospital.

In 1963 she married a young Navaho, Alexander Evans, who was on his tour of duty with the army. When her husband was sent to Panama, Nancy returned to her parents' home at Beclabito until after the birth of her daughter. By that time the situation in Panama was such that families of service men were

*Herbert Blatchford in the field.*

*At work as a counselor.*

*Nancy Rose Benally when a student at the University of New Mexico.*

*Anthropologist Shirley Sells as a ranger at Canyon de Chelly.*

not permitted to join their husbands. Until the young man's release from the army, Nancy Rose worked with the New Mexico State Welfare Department at Shiprock. Following Alexander Evans' return to his family, he and Nancy Rose moved to Window Rock to assume work for a new tribal project, positions they both still hold. With Nancy Rose's knowledge, ability, and experience, the future should hold promise for a position where her talents can be used to the full.

Nancy Rose's parents are fine old-type Navaho who, though they speak but little English, passed on their capacities to an able daughter. This young woman is a superlative example of the Navaho ability to learn new ways and a new kind of life, yet retain the best of traditional ways.

A third honor student receiving an Education Scholarship Fund Grant is Shirley Sells. Shirley, now twenty-four, was born in Shiprock and received her elementary schooling through the tenth grade in Gallup. Then she spent a year in California with a teacher whom she knew, going to school there. Returning to the reservation, she graduated from the Window Rock High School, and went on to the University of New Mexico, where she majored in anthropology and speech, receiving her diploma in June, 1964.

During the summer months of 1963 and 1964 Shirley held a position as a ranger in the National Park Service, stationed at Canyon de Chelly National Monument. In all spare moments she has been working on a thesis in archaeology. Following the summer season of 1964 at the Canyon, Shirley accepted a position with a survey sponsored jointly by the Navaho Tribe and the Bureau of Indian Affairs. She is working also at the Arizona State University on a two-year award from the Department of Anthropology as a graduate assistant, and in addition is studying genetics and animal ecology. It is altogether fitting that

*Men leaving Gallup for work on the railroad.*

there should be a Navaho anthropologist, and I am sure that Shirley will perform a major service for her people in recording and preserving the traditions and folklore of the Navaho.

These are but three of the honor students who either have been, or are being, helped through the Scholarship Fund. There are many others, following a variety of occupations, such as doctors, dentists, nurses, and lawyers, all of them bringing back to their own people the benefits of their learning, for a stipulation with each grant is that the student must devote a minimum of two years' service to the Tribe following the completion of his work.

This Education Scholarship Fund is probably the most valuable of all the Navaho projects, giving many young people of ability the opportunity to receive the highest education. From this group will doubtless come the leaders of tomorrow. That the Tribal Council had the wisdom to establish such a fund shows again the ability of these people to make practical decisions for the benefit of the Tribe. Many of these councilmen were older men who had not had such opportunities themselves and who were willing to plan far ahead for the future of their people.

During the past thirty years, it has become more and more necessary for young Navaho men and women to seek employment off the reservation. Those who had learned to speak English were the first to do so. For many years now, both the Santa Fe and the Union Pacific railroads have employed Navaho men for maintenance work along their lines, and occasionally one may see them boarding a train for work at some distant point. Many other Navaho go into off-reservation parts of New Mexico, Arizona, Utah, and Colorado for seasonal crop harvesting. A

*A young man operating large road-building equipment.*

*Agnes Draper, a skilled typist.*

*A waitress in a Gallup restaurant.*

good many young women find employment of various kinds in restaurants or motels in the nearby towns. Many also have studied typing and have taken the place of former Indian Service typists at Window Rock, where they have proved to be efficient and skilled office workers.

The Indian Service has made some effort to relocate families, which has been partially successful, some Navaho moving to California, Colorado, the larger cities of New Mexico and Arizona, and even farther afield where they have found satisfactory work for their livelihood.

As many of the new projects on the reservation have developed, more opportunities for Navaho People have arisen at home, such as work in road building, in the oil fields, in the uranium mines, in the Sawmill project, and in other lines of endeavor replacing the sheep industry on the overused land. Mechanical ability seems to be natural to all young Navaho boys, and they find work in garages along the border towns of the reservation. It is interesting to see the skill with which these young men handle big machinery, so far removed from the old life of a generation ago.

*Law and Order*

The development of the Department of Law and Order has been slow, for traditionally every individual Nahavo is a free agent and no one should try to impose his will upon another. For many years there were few serious offences, and those that did occur were usually handled by the headman of each clan. As disputes among the Navaho were relatively minor, they were settled by arbitration.

In 1880, acting Navaho Agent Bennet said in his report to Washington:

> The crying evil that most besets this people is whisky. There are several traders at nearby points . . . where whisky of the vilest description is delt out to these people in open violation of the law, being an incentive to crime and greatly impoverishing many of them. . . . Outside of this aspect of the question no community of like population will exhibit so small a record of criminal acts of a flagrant character as the Navahoes.[2]

Even today the high percentage of arrests are due to problem drinking; other misdemeanors are relatively few.

[2] *Navajo Yearbook*, p. 275.

*Captain William Yellowhair, Navaho Police Force, Tuba City.*

The Bureau of Indian Affairs was responsible for the maintenance of law and order on the reservation until 1953 when the need for a tribal police force became acute in the Checkerboard Area, off the reservation. The state of New Mexico could not handle these Indian problems and asked for help from the Tribe. This area has long been a veritable no man's land as far as policing was concerned. For example, bootleggers from surrounding communities went to the area with quantities of cheap liquor, selling it to the Indians and demanding the immediate return of bottles so that no evidence was left behind. The state agreed to help police this area if its force were augmented, so six Navaho policemen were trained and equipped for the work. These men were the beginning of the Navaho Police Force. It has grown steadily since, and today there are approximately two hundred enforcement officers with sufficient administrative personnel.

*Judge Hadley's court at Tuba City.*

Now there are seven courts, one in each subagency and two at Window Rock, conducted entirely by Navaho judges and officers. I had the very interesting experience in being present at a court session at Tuba City. I do not know what offense the young man had committed, but I was impressed with the conduct of the court, and with Judge Hadley's handling of the prisoner. The Judge gave the boy a long talk, which of course I could not understand. But I could understand the quality of his voice and the meaning of his words by the inflection of his voice and the manner in which he spoke. His voice was persuasive rather than dictatorial, kind rather than harsh or critical, and I felt that the boy was being taught rather than admonished. The whole procedure was quiet, reserved, sincere, and dignified. I wished that George Washington, looking down from the wall, might have heard this session.

The Tribe has just completed a wonderful new Law and Order Building, situated within the Window Rock grounds. This is a handsome building of modern design containing the last word in police and prison facilities. On the second floor are two courtrooms with adequate chambers for the judges, a law library, and the finest of modern equipment.

Whenever new projects are commenced by the

*Navaho woman and children gather scant fodder for their sheep in the Checkerboard Area.*

Tribe, the Council sends for top-ranking experts to give advice on the best possible ways to proceed. They call in expert architects, engineers, lawyers, geologists, and men of other professions, their judgment being always to seek the very best. Following the creation of the Indian Land Claims Commission by the Congress of the United States in 1946, the Tribal Council, under the chairmanship of Sam Ahkeah, passed a resolution to employ an attorney to function both as claims attorney and as general counsel. Sam went to Washington to secure the services of Mr. Norman M. Littell, a prominent corporation lawyer, and a ten-year contract with him was approved by the Council in July of 1947. As the new mining activities developed, the need arose for continued legal counsel at Window Rock; consequently, in 1951 the Tribal Council acted to employ a resident attorney to function under Mr. Littell's direction. In order to obtain the maximum benefits for the Navaho People, highly competent advice was necessary to execute not only mining, oil, and gas leases, but also many agreements in connection with the Glen Canyon Dam, the rights of way for power lines, and much other business that has recently come to the Tribe. In addition to the general counsel, a Department of Tribal Legal Aid has been added, to render service to individuals whose interests need protection.

During the period of work on the land claims, I joined archaeologist Richard Van Valkenburgh at a meeting held in the eastern part of the Checkerboard Area, where he was seeking help from older Navaho men in his effort to locate Old Navaholand hogan sites where the Navaho lived nearly four centuries ago. It was a bitterly cold day and, as the heating plant was not in operation in the building where the meeting was to have taken place, everyone

*The meeting at Counselor, New Mexico.*

*In the dry Checkerboard Area, where the going is rough.*

crowded into a hogan to listen to a talk by Mr. Counselor, formerly a trader in the area. Men, women, and children were present, all listening attentively to the problem at hand. Luckily I had permission to record this scene. Two elderly Navaho men finally agreed to help Mr. Van Valkenburgh the following summer, at which time I again joined the group to watch the work in progress. Some old sites were found near our camp, and from the logs valuable tree-ring data were obtained. One of the men who helped was Georgie Garcia (p. 37), who at seventy-eight was still surprisingly active. Much archaeological evidence was gained that summer to establish proof of Navaho habitation in areas no longer within the present reservation boundary.

The land claims work is finished now and awaits the decision of the United States Supreme Court.

### The Checkerboard Area

East of the present boundary of the Navaho Reservation is the land known as the Checkerboard Area, where disputes over land ownership have prevailed for many years. When the Navaho People returned from Fort Sumner in 1868 many of them, regardless of the government-decreed reservation boundaries, drifted naturally to their former homes where they and their forebears had lived for many generations. Some of these homes were in this eastern area. By 1875 some non-Indian sheep men in New Mexico began to graze their stock where the Navaho lived. Disputes over ownership arose as fences were built to keep Navaho stock away from water sources they had long used.

When the Santa Fe Railroad was being built in 1882 some portions of the right-of-way crossed the southern portion of the reservation proper. Here the federal government granted to the railroad every other section of land on both sides of the track, taking away from the Navaho much of their good grazing areas. Under the leadership of Manuelito, a group of headmen went to Washington to plead with President Grant for the return of this land, but to no avail. Other land north of the San Juan River was offered instead. However, some exchanges did occur in a few regions, leading to the naming of this large area as the Checkerboard. Various efforts to make adjustments were attempted during the ensuing years, backed by several non-Indians who had fair dealing at heart, but land speculators managed to defeat these efforts.

At the time of the Homestead Act in 1916 the Navaho People could have filed for this land, but who was there to explain to the People who had lived on this land for generations that they must establish legal claim? Within the Checkerboard Area 49 percent of the land was Navaho owned, 20 percent was under federal control, 16 percent was owned by the railroad, 7 percent was state land, 3 percent was owned by the New Mexico-Arizona Land Company, and 4 percent was privately owned by non-Indians.

Secretary of the Interior Harold L. Ickes withdrew the entire four million acres of the Checkerboard Area from entry in this disputed area. Between 1933 and 1935 the governor of New Mexico and Senators Bronson Cutting and Carl Hatch prepared an act to define these reservation boundaries. The bill passed the Senate in 1935, but before it reached the House of Representatives, Senator Cutting was killed in an airplane accident. As he had been the chief proponent of this bill, the opposition was now able to cause its withdrawal for reconsideration, with the end result that the bill was dropped. Through the Arizona Boundary Bill (1934), some land along the southern boundary of the reservation in Arizona was purchased by the federal government and added to the reservation. In New Mexico, however, some disputed land still exists, and in the meantime the Navaho Tribe

*In the pine forest of the Chuska Mountains.*

*The old lumber plant at Sawmill was out in the open.*

has purchased several large ranches. It is certainly to be hoped that the Indian Service will be able eventually to restore land areas to which the Navaho have an inherited claim.

*Tribal Resources*

When the Tribal Council voted in 1940 to establish a Department of Resources, the first two resources on the list were the Sawmill Project (which had been in limited operation previously) and the Arts and Crafts Guild. There are many thousand acres of fine timber on the reservation in the Chuska Mountains, and in smaller amounts elsewhere. With the supervision of the Forest Division of the Bureau of Indian Affairs, the Sawmill Project was commenced at a site some forty miles northwest of Window Rock. Selected trees were cut and brought to the mill, where some two hundred Navaho men were trained in the best methods of handling lumber and in the concept of sustained yield forestry. Over eighteen million board feet of lumber were produced per annum at this original site. With expanded industry in sight, a

*Monument Valley.*

*Looking west to the Monument Valley silhouette from the desert area near the uranium mines. Navaho Mountain is in the distance.*

*A worker in a uranium mine on top of the Lukachukai Mountains.*

*Sorting uranium ore at the Shiprock processing plant.*

new location was selected and an up-to-date mill with modern equipment was built some fifteen miles northeast of Fort Defiance. This new mill has more than doubled the capacity of the former plant, and today there are more than four hundred Navaho men employed at the mill and some forty-odd non-Navaho. A small housing area called Navajo has been built for these people near the mill. This industry is netting the Tribe an income of several hundred thousand dollars a year.

The discovery of uranium ore on the reservation in 1950 sent a wave of excitement throughout the Southwest. Much prospecting was done, and more sources of ore both large and small were located with an eager rush reminiscent of the old gold mining days. Roads were both improved and newly built in order to haul ore by truck to the processing plant at Shiprock. When more ore was discovered in the Monument Valley area and farther west, two additional plants were built, one at Mexican Hat and another at Tuba City. The vast barren desert east of the Monuments provided unsuspected riches for the Navaho Tribe as well as work for many men, for here a large open-pit mine was operated. On the top of the northern

*An oil pumping station near the Four Corners.*

*Much Navaho wealth comes from oil.*

end of the Lukachukai Mountains several shaft mines yielded many thousand tons of uranium ores. I visited one of these and was taken down into the mine, where it seemed strange indeed to find Navaho boys deep underground hard at work as miners. The peak year of the uranium mining was reached in 1962 when some 379,000 tons of ore were produced, adding immense revenue to the tribal treasury.

Though the first oil was struck on the reservation as long ago as 1921 when the Rattlesnake dome was discovered near Shiprock, new fields were found in 1957, also in this northern district of the San Juan River basin, particularly in the Four Corners area. More than one thousand new oil and gas wells are now operating, bringing in high revenue. The first years of production from these new fields brought in many millions of dollars in leases and bonuses, while the annual royalty of some twelve million dollars is of prime importance to the Tribe.

Another recent development has been a strip coal mining site, south of the San Juan River between Shiprock and Farmington. This coal is being converted into power at the site, and a new power line now extends over the Chuska Mountains to the Window Rock area and beyond, bringing electricity for many purposes.

The Glen Canyon area is offering other new developments. Generated by the giant turbines at the new dam, great pylons carry the pulsing rhythm of electric power for 150 miles across the desert. This source of power will be tapped in the future when the need for it arises.

On the whole, the recent rich earnings from the Department of Resources are being wisely used. On some Indian reservations where sudden large sums of money were received, the money was distributed to the individuals. This resulted in quick expenditure. The Navaho not only have made good investments, but also have used funds to develop programs of many sorts created for the benefit of all the Navaho People. Having known for nearly twenty years some of the individuals who now hold responsible positions, I find it most heartening to see how they have risen to the challenge of their respective departments, and to see the ability they are showing in executive posts. Certainly they seem to have the good of the Tribe as a whole at heart.

# THE FAIRS

FORTY-FIVE YEARS AGO, a group of citizens in Gallup, New Mexico, conceived the idea of having an annual fair for the benefit of the several Indian tribes who lived in the general area. This developed into the Inter-tribal Ceremonial, which during the course of the past twenty-five years has become a renowned affair. The original idea of an arts and crafts exhibit where the Indians could sell their work now has grown into an outstanding exhibition with Indians from many tribes competing for a variety of prizes. In the last decade Indians have come from all over the United States, parts of British Columbia, and Mexico to take part in the Ceremonial in one way or another, bringing added color, interest, and variety.

In addition to the crafts exhibits, there are many other forms of competition and entertainment. The members of the Gallup Ceremonial Committee, finding that some dances by Southwestern Indians were on the verge of disappearing, offered special prizes for their revival. While all dances are part of religious ceremonials, the presentation of some as isolated units seems to be permissible. These dramatic event's take place at the fairgrounds before a capacity-filled grandstand for all performances, while additional spectators seek every possible vantage point to witness both afternoon and evening events. During the daytime there are athletic competitions of many sorts; with these and the evening entertainments, the four days of the Ceremonial are filled with a variety of interesting things to watch. The Navaho play an important part in the Ceremonial, for they lead the opening parade, carrying the flags and partaking in all the equestrian events.

Another aspect of this Ceremonial is the social

*The Navaho gather on the hill for the Gallup Ceremonial.*

gathering of the many tribes. Here they exchange knowledge and thoughts with one another, discussing all manner of work and events, for the Gallup Ceremonial has done much to weld the Indian peoples of all tribes together. These four days in mid-August are filled with color, with action, with gaiety and social pleasures. To the non-Indian spectators this is doubtless one of the most colorful affairs in the country; and it can be a field day for photographers, with action of many sorts, as well as moments of dramatic performances and of human interest.

As early as 1909, agricultural agent William T. Shelton instigated a fair, like any county fair, at Shiprock for the benefit of the northern Navaho area. He did much to encourage superior weaving through this fair, promoting displays of rugs. For a while the fair was discontinued, to be resumed in 1937 with increased emphasis on weaving, as well as agricultural and livestock exhibits, for Mr. Shelton did much to improve the quality of Navaho sheep, and consequently wool, in this part of the reservation. The Shiprock Fair, of course, is an all-Navaho event, held usually in early October. While the original purpose of this fair was the display of agricultural produce with prizes for the top-ranking exhibits as well as livestock, this is also an educational fair, for here the

*Awaiting the entry at the Gallup Intertribal Ceremony.*

*Behind the scenes at the Gallup Ceremonial.*

many farmers learn how to improve their produce and livestock.

Other exhibits will also be found at this fair, such as home economic exhibits with canned fruits and vegetables and other exhibits from the woman's world. In the small arena a variety of equestrian activities take place, for Navaho youths have become eager participants in all rodeo events. Though the Navaho are natural sheep men, they are also fine horsemen, and during the past twenty years have become excellent rodeo performers. I recall watching a calf-roping contest in the early 1950's when the best time for the event was over sixty seconds; but at a recent fair I saw a boy win this contest with a time of eleven seconds.

A few years ago, a small traveling carnival made its appearance at the Shiprock Fair. Here were the usual lot of booths with throwing contests, a Ferris wheel, and other rides, all of which were eagerly enjoyed by all ages. Somehow the Shiprock Fair, though much smaller than the others, is more fun, perhaps because it is less sophisticated and pretentious, though recently the drinking problem has been much too evident.

In 1938, not long after the establishment of the

*Onlookers at the Gallup Ceremonial.*

*Outside the exhibit area at the Shiprock Fair.*

*A family argument at the Shiprock Fair.*

*Rodeo events at Shiprock Fair.*

*The Grand Entry at the Window Rock Fair.*

*The Window Rock arena, 1953.*

*The Window Rock arena, 1964.*

Navaho seat of government at Window Rock, the Tribal Council voted to mount a tribal fair. Grounds were laid out not far from the government buildings, and for four years the fair was conducted in September. During World War II, this fair was suspended, to be reactivated in 1951. Since then it has grown in scope and activity, and is now the big event on the reservation. Modeled somewhat after the Gallup Ceremonial, the fair always has a fine craft exhibit, and large displays of agricultural exhibits in the new Gorman Hall. There are excellent quarters for the livestock displays and facilities for judging the specimens which come in from all parts of the reservation. There is a race track surrounding the rodeo arena (they even have a mechanical race starter), a loud speaker system, and all modern equipment. The spacious grandstand holds many spectators. The opening event in this arena is one of many galloping horses, as the Navaho young men ride in with the band playing and flags flying. This is also a four-day fair, with new daily events and competitions in the arena. One interesting contest is for women to see who can chop wood and light a fire in the shortest time. There are also evening events, small bits from ceremonials, dances by visiting Pueblo dancers, and other events to interest the spectators.

The beautiful new Community Building is opened at fair time for educational and commercial exhibits,

*Shiprock Fair.*

*Overlooking the fairgrounds from the Community Center.*

*The Community Center.*

showing the latest farming machinery, new trucks, and all sorts of house and farm utensils. There are short educational movies, such as a film on tuberculosis, and one on Alcoholics Anonymous, which it is interesting to see crowds of young men watching. School exhibits are displayed here, and subscriptions to *The Navajo Times*, a weekly publication in English, are sold at a booth.

The Community Center Building has many unique features: it can be partitioned off into classrooms, it can be made into a sports area for boxing and wrestling, it can be made into two basketball courts (a game well loved and well played by the Navaho boys), and it can also be turned into an auditorium or concert hall with tiered removable seats. At the dedication ceremonies, a famous troupe of Spanish dancers performed here, to the delight of the Navaho audience. José Iturbi played here, and there have been other concerts of equally high quality. Some of the great jazz bands have given concerts here, as each year brings a growing list of important cultural presentations.

Recently, since the erection of the new Arts and Crafts Guild Building, the old one at the fairgrounds has been made into a small museum containing many exhibits of year-round interest. A small children's zoo has been added to the south of the building, containing wild animals and birds found on the reservation.

The Gallup Ceremonial, the Fourth of July celebration at Flagstaff, the Shiprock Fair, and the Window Rock Tribal Fair are all widely attended by hundreds, probably thousands, of Navaho people, as well as Indians of other tribes and countless non-Indian visitors. These gatherings give the Navaho people the opportunity to discuss the affairs of the day and work that is being done. Many Navaho who live far from the reservation come home for one or more of these events, where they may see their families and friends and renew their Navaho traditions.

# PART IV

# THE ENDURING WAY

# HERITAGE

When the Dinéh, the Earth People, emerged into this world, they were taught by the Holy People the right way to conduct the many acts of their everyday living—how to gain a livelihood, how to build a hogan, how to perform the myriad activities of their lives, and, above all, how to adapt to their environment for good or evil through the harmonious use of ceremonials. Springing from the Creation Story, in which the development of man is established, the legends contain the origins of the ceremonies, the answers to fundamental questions, and the reasons for the many taboos. There seems to be no clearly defined supreme being in Navaho thought; however, there is the knowledge that through ceremonial rituals certain of the Yei (the Holy Ones) can be encouraged to assist with supernatural powers. It is the Yei who regulate whether good or evil comes to the Dinéh; but not all the Yei are good, thus there is constant supplication to win favor of the good Yei, and to override the influences of the evil.

Misfortune, accident, and illness are caused by disharmony, either direct or through social controls known as witchcraft, and every effort is made to overcome these and to propitiate and create perfect harmony with the good. This is accomplished through the complex and intricate patterns of ceremonialism. Performed by the esoteric medicine men who have the knowledge and the influence, these ceremonials are the embodiment of natural consequences and abstract symbolism, expressed through song, through the dry paintings (sand paintings), and through the correct use of ceremonial objects and substances.

When a patient is uncertain in determining which ceremony is necessary to produce the required heal-

*A medicine man with his paraphernalia.*

ing, there are diagnosticians who perform this service—these are the hand tremblers, the star gazers, and the listeners who consult the patient and, through their ability, determine the course to follow.

When it has been decided which ceremony is to be given, the medicine man, or singer, as he is more correctly called, who knows that particular ceremony is summoned and preparations are set in motion. Stemming from the Creation Story, more than fifty ceremonies, or chants, of varying range and complexity all lead to the restoration of harmony. Everything must be done in the prescribed way as told in the legends. So it is the spiritual, emotional, psychological, and physical needs, *and in this order*, that are treated to attain this desired harmony and, consequently, healing.

The most revered ceremony, a relatively simple one, is the Blessingway, the Hozhoji, the center of Navaho religion, in which Changing Woman plays a predominant part. This does not require the elaborate ritual of most of the other ceremonies, and may be performed by anyone who knows it. As its name implies, it is an act of balance, a blessing for a person, a place, or an act, such as the commencing of a new blanket, and it comes from Changing Woman, regenerator of life, the everlasting One.

Many smaller rites, such as the puberty ceremony, the initiation ceremony, the marriage ceremony, and ceremonials, such as the Mountainway or the Night-numerous others are conducted frequently. The great way, with their variations, are less frequently given. As these particular ceremonies last for nine days and nights, they are very costly affairs requiring much preparation, but others are of shorter duration. While the first days of these long chants usually concern only the patient and family, it is on the ninth day that great numbers of people come from far and near to watch the ceremony of the final night and to partake of its benefits.

During these large ceremonials, sand paintings are executed within a hogan often specially built for the rituals. Directed by the singer, his helpers create the proper design by trickling sand of different colors through their fingers onto a base of neutral-colored sand spread over the hogan floor. Commenced in the morning, the painting is completed in mid-afternoon, when the patient is brought in and placed upon it. The medicine man then takes sand from certain symbolic sections of the design, and rubs it onto the patient to absorb the causes of the illness. When these rites are completed, the entire sand painting is wiped out, but during that brief time when it lies complete on the hogan floor it is an extraordinarily beautiful example of abstract art, every part of which is replete with significance. Hundreds of these designs, some completely abstract, some partially pictorial, all with different purposes, are stored in the memories of the medicine men who direct their execution. Many contain the stylized symbolic figures of some of the Yei, the sun and the moon, or some of the helpers of both gods and men, such as Big Fly (the messenger), Coyote, Bear (which the Navaho revere), or other animals and birds. In many sand paintings one sees the Four Sacred Plants—corn, squash, beans, and tobacco—drawn in decorative designs. Many paint-

*Sand painting.*

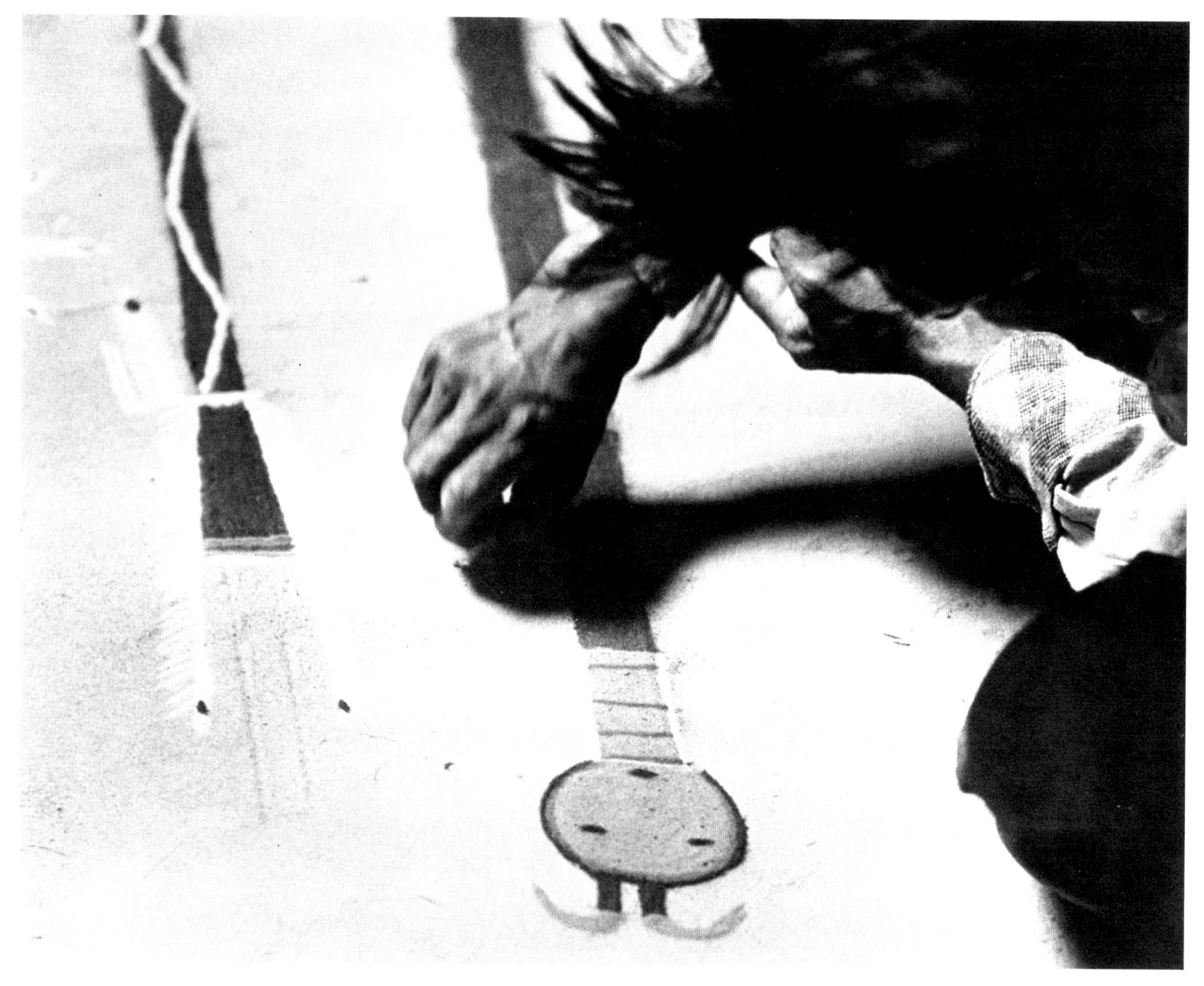

ings are encircled by the Rainbow Goddess for protection, the opening (for there is never a complete enclosure) always to the East; some are encircled with entwined serpents, some with a simple border.

Native pigments are used in making these remarkable designs. For some ceremonies, such as Blessingway, vegetable pigments are used—crushed petals from flowers, pollens, cornmeal, and pulverized charcoal for black. In the large sand paintings the pigments are crushed red sandstone, yellow ochre, white gypsum, and charcoal made from burnt scrub oak. In the Nightway the black must be made from dry cedar charcoal. A grey blue is obtained by mixing white sand or gypsum with charcoal, a pink from a mixture of red sandstone and white, a brown by mixing yellow ochre and charcoal. Pieces of bark are used as trays to hold each color, though today one sees paper plates or cups as receptacles. The making of these paintings is done with skill and certainty by many helpers as the pigments trickle from between their thumbs and forefingers in steady strokes.

At the great ceremonials there will be as many as

five different sand paintings on ensuing days, each with its special ritual at the end—all part of the healing ceremony which moves steadily forward in its prescribed order to the climax of the final night.

*The Mountainway*

In the late fall of 1932, Betsy sent me word that there was to be a Fire Dance at Lukachukai, and that she hoped I would be able to join her, as she expected to go with a number of Navaho people from her area. The Fire Dance, she wrote, was the final night of the Mountainway. She suggested that I arrive early in November, as she was not certain of the date. The day after my arrival we set forth in our respective cars, Betsy taking five Navaho with her, I taking four with me.

We drove up over the Lukachukai Mountains from Red Rock, arriving at the location in the afternoon of the eighth day of the ceremony. And what a sight greeted us! We found ourselves near the base of the great red sandstone cliffs which jut out into the broad expanse known as the Chinle Wash. Rich green piñon and cedar trees were scattered along the base of the cliffs, and where the slope dropped, soft grey-green sagebrush took their place. We put up our tent on the outskirts of the activity, Timothy eagerly helping us.

He was full of excitement, for he had never seen a Fire Dance. We spent the afternoon watching all the preparations for the day and night to follow. Near us was a huge shelter, newly constructed, where busy cooks were already preparing food for the entire assembly. Here we learned that the patient giving the ceremony and his family furnished food for all who come. It is customary, however, for visitors to contribute to the supply by bringing flour, sugar, or coffee, and we were most courteously thanked for our donations. We watched the butchering of sheep and goats, saw huge kettles being prepared for cooking mutton and goat meat, saw specially constructed stone and mud ovens where women were baking great quantities of bread. We saw men hauling water, and men hauling wood, not only for the cooking fires, but for the ceremonial fires during the night to follow. We watched the making of a great wood pile near the ceremonial hogan. It seemed large enough to last an entire winter for a whole community; yet it was completely consumed the following night. As we came near the hogan we heard the voices of the singers as they performed the eighth-day rituals. We were afraid we might displease our host if we approached, so we listened from afar. It never occurred to us that we might have asked to see the ceremony, and that possibly we might have been invited to watch.

As evening came, a crowd gathered, standing in a circle to watch rehearsals for the dance to be performed the following night. This lasted for some time, then there was silence as a man stepped out into the center near the firelight. In his high-pitched voice, which carried easily for considerable distance, he spoke long and earnestly, then suddenly we heard two familiar words, *Washingdon* [sic] and *Roosevelt.* We had forgotten that it was election day; it was strangely wonderful to hear the election returns in another language so far removed in thought and feeling from twentieth-century America. Then the singing resumed and finally we crept into our sleeping bags, falling asleep before the singing ended.

A bustle of excitement filled the air the next morning; after our breakfast, we watched a crew of men bringing in freshly cut cedar and piñon boughs and constructing a huge circle, or corral, near the ceremonial hogan. They stacked the boughs more than six feet high, intertwining the branches and completing the circle, except for the entrance to the East. The corral must have been more than two hundred feet in diameter, the boughs so closely interwoven that little wind came through. One crew brought long dry logs, stacking them on end in the center of the corral for the bonfire to be lighted later in the night. So absorbed were we in watching this that we had not looked about us, but suddenly we were aware of fresh activity, and looking up we saw Navaho people coming from all directions—down through the trees, up from the valley, in covered wagons, on horseback, in open wagons, in a few cars. Most came in family groups, some singly on horseback or on foot; all were dressed in their very best, the women with freshly washed long full cotton skirts and beautiful blouses of reds, blues, purples, yellows, and greens, filling the landscape like a kaleidoscope. Never before or since have I seen anything to equal the color of that day, with the great red cliffs as a background for this medley of color moving through the changing greens of the foreground as this gathering of the Dinéh assembled. All day long they came, tethering their horses, greeting one another by the quiet, gentle handclasp so distinctly Navaho, partaking of the food prepared and constantly renewed within the cook shelter.

As the sun fell behind the distant mesas, the singer emerged from the hogan, followed by his assistants. Taking his medicine pouch from his belt, he commenced sprinkling corn pollen as he entered the corral, moving slowly clockwise around the circle, singing the Blessing Song, in which the others joined. As he returned to the hogan the people began to move into the corral, finding places for themselves, some close to the green walls of branches, some in front, forming an audience several rows deep. We entered too, Timothy finding a place for us where we would be able to watch the night's proceedings. We had brought blankets with us, for the evening was cold, and we settled down to watch. Soon there were little fires all about, lighted for warmth, and with a coffee pot always close by.

Just at dark, when the ritual was finished in the hogan, the medicine man, his helpers, and the patient came out, and entered the corral to take their places at the westernmost side of the circle, where they turned to face the East. A pathway was kept clear between them and the great bonfire, soon to be

lighted. A group of singers came in, each with a rattle in his hand, dancing around the bonfire as it was ignited, quickly illuminating the scene. When these dancers had completed their prescribed group of songs, others entered to take their places, so that the singing never ceased. To this ebb and flow of dance and song, the special events of the night were added from time to time—the tricksters who made yucca grow before your eyes, and who performed other magic tricks, a girl who danced before a basket containing a single feather which rose on end in the basket, swaying slightly with the rhythm of the song.

Years later at the Gallup Ceremonial, we saw again one of the special events from the Fire Dance. The dimly lit singers kneeled before the fire, while dancers carried great frames or wands decorated with eagle feathers and symbolic eagles riding high above symbolic suns. This recalled vividly the night we had spent at Lukachukai, so long ago.

As the night wore on, a group of four fire dancers came into the corral, each carrying a long strand of cedar bark which in turn they ignited at the bonfire, then as they dashed madly around the blazing logs they flayed both themselves and each other with the burning bark. They were clad only in breech cloths, their bodies painted with a light-colored clay which must have been very heat resistant. Another special event of the night was performed by two of these dancers. One lifted a piece of burning pitchy wood from the fire, holding it over the cupped hands of the other dancer who washed his hands in the dripping burning pitch. Doubtless there were other events which have now faded from my memory, but what impressed me the most throughout that mysterious night was the sight of those wonderful firelit faces of the People as they sat wrapped in their blankets watching the sequence of events that took place.

During the night the aromatic fragrance of burning piñon and cedar wood filled the air, and occasional gusts of wind blew smoke in our eyes, stinging them greatly. One family, patients of Betsy's, saw us sitting there, and, thinking we had nothing to eat, brought us boiled mutton and coffee. They all gave us welcome, considering our comfort as we watched the unfolding drama. There must have been several hundred children there that night, but not once did we hear a child or baby cry. All were absorbed as long as they could stay awake, then they slept quietly until they were rested.

Just before the dawn came, a great lot of logs were thrown on the ebbing fire, and as the first signs of breaking day appeared over the cliffs, the fire dancers came rushing in for the last time. Snatching burning strips of bark from the fire, they first circled it four times, then, running to throw the burning strips over the corral wall in each of the four directions, they broke open the wall to the South, the West, and the North, so that all could leave the corral in the direction in which they lived.

As the sun came up, lighting the crests of the red cliffs and soon sending rays of sunlight across the scene, we watched the People preparing to return to their homes. Finally I timidly got out a camera to make a few pictures of groups near us as they loaded their wagons and harnessed their horses. We treasure the memory of that night, the vision of those wonderful faces, the spirit that emanated from them, and the friendliness of these people so filled with the benediction of their experience that it gave us a deep insight into Navaho character. More than eighteen hundred people were there that night and only five or six non-Indian visitors, including ourselves. Never had we been in such a large gathering where all the people were so well behaved, for at this time, 1932, there were no problems of alcoholism that too often appear at ceremonials today. Only recently I found a trader who had been present that night and he told me that, of all the many ceremonials he had seen during a period of forty years on the reservation, that night's was the finest he had ever seen.

The summer after we saw the great Fire Dance, Betsy wrote me that she was going to spend several weeks camped on the mountain above Red Rock, as many of her people were there with their sheep for summer pasture, and there had been an epidemic of influenza. She came down to Red Rock to meet me, and after stocking up with supplies at the trading post we drove to a lovely meadow where she had previously pitched her tent.

We took a walk across the meadow where we found some edible mushrooms, which we eagerly gathered to improve a steak we had brought for supper. As we were returning to the campsite we suddenly saw a silent figure standing at the edge of the woods watch-

*The medicine man up on the mountain.*

*A medicine woman.*

*A modern medicine man and his children.*

ing us. He proved to be a medicine man of Betsy's acquaintance who greeted us with quiet reserve and walked back with us to our camp. A sudden summer thunderstorm broke loose, and with Timothy joining us we took shelter under the tent fly to await the passing of the storm.

Moved by a spirit of friendliness, the medicine man asked Betsy if she would like to see his medicine pouch. We watched with interest as he untied the buckskin thongs, greatly worn from long use, and laid out the contents before us. For a medicine bowl he had a turtle shell in which he mixed the herb remedies he carried in a number of small leather bags. This shell had been given him by a very old medicine man who had used it all his life. It was cracked and it leaked; our friend asked Betsy if she could get him another. (This I was able to send her after my return home.) Then there were two strange objects which turned out to be the skulls of wild cranes. We had seen the bills of these bird heads protruding from the pouch. The neck ends were bound with colored worsted and decorated with feathers and small bits of shell. These, we were to learn later, were part of the special paraphernalia required for the Knife Chant, one of the rituals practiced by this man. There were also prayer sticks, special bags of corn pollen, some fetishes, some stones from the sacred mountains, and a few other objects. We were very interested to see all of this collection and to see the reverence with which the medicine man handled his ritualistic possessions.

Somehow our conversation (and this all through Timothy, Betsy's interpreter) drifted to telling stories. I cannot remember what prompted us to tell the Greek tale of the Gorgon's Head, but after the tale was told, the medicine man asked Timothy to tell us that the Navaho had a story something like that; he wished he could tell it to us, but it was forbidden to tell it in the summertime when it thundered and he must wait until after the first frost; besides, it would have taken three days and three nights to tell. As Betsy never did find the opportunity to hear the story, this is one of the countless folk tales of the Navaho we do not know.

When the storm was over, we were ready to cook our evening meal, and we invited our visitor to join us. I broiled the steak over an open fire, cooked the mushrooms, and served what I thought was an excellent meal. But the steak was too rare for Navaho taste, and neither Timothy nor the medicine man would touch the mushrooms; somewhat crestfallen, we endeavored to find something else more to their liking.

*The Blessingway*

In addition to the blessing of every new hogan, the Blessingway ceremony is also conducted whenever a new building is completed on the reservation. At the time of the opening of the large new school at Crownpoint, I went over for the occasion. There were many visitors, both non-Indian and Navaho, gathering for the dedication ceremonies, and there was much preparation of food.

As the scheduled hour approached, the school children marched into the new building, joining the visitors to form a large semicircle just inside the western door of the main entrance hall. Then rugs were placed on the floor, the medicine man (Manuelito Begay) and three other singers took their places on the rugs, the ceremonial basket containing sacred corn pollen and a special pouch holding stones from the four sacred mountains was placed before them, and their chanting began. There are no special features to this ceremony, only the reverent, simple prayers of benediction for the use of the building and the blessing of those who participate in its activities.

In all ceremonies one must leave by the exit to the East (should there be one in any other direction). At this ceremony Herbert Blatchford was present, and when it was finished I saw Herbert step quickly behind the chanters to lock the western door so that no one could use it. Then all went out through the door to the East to the courtyard, where chairs and benches had been placed for the dedication ceremony to be conducted by the school officials. The school band played, the children took their places, parents and visitors found theirs, and the usual ceremony for such occasions took place.

When this was over, the Navaho lingered to talk before going to have their feast. It was here that we watched women making fry bread in the most enormous skillets I have ever seen. A spirit of gaiety was present, with everyone having a wonderful time as great quantities of fry bread melted away and gallons of coffee disappeared.

*Making fry bread at Blessingway, Crownpoint.*

*The blessing ceremony at Crownpoint school.*

*Making fry bread for the Crownpoint ceremony.*

*Navaho gathering for a Squaw Dance (1934).*

*The Enemyway*

Betsy and I have been privileged to witness some ceremonies in part only, but from these experiences we have realized the great mass of intricate ritual that each ceremony contains. To learn or even to witness portions of them all would take a lifetime, and there are probably but few non-Indians who could fathom the often delicate and subtle differences, the significant symbolism, the true meaning that these rituals have for the Navaho People. But we can comprehend the beauty of many of the ceremonies that we are permitted to see, and become aware of the reverent feeling that exists among not only those conducting the rituals but also all those who attend. From such experiences we can realize how deeply the Navaho are concerned with the proper ordering of life in this world, and the traditional ethics which guide human relationships.

Perhaps the most frequently given ceremony is the so-called Squaw Dance, also called the War Dance, though its real name is The Enemyway. This is a three-day ceremony stemming from the legend of Changing Woman's twin sons, Monster Slayer and Child-of-the-Water, who went to visit their father, the Sun, to seek his aid that they might slay the monsters who inhabited this earth in order to make it a safe place for the Dinéh to live. After slaying the monster Yeitso, the twins carried his scalp as a trophy, hanging it on a tree before telling their mother of their adventure. While relating their story to her, they swooned and lay unconscious. Changing Woman prepared a potion made of herbs which had been struck by lightning, sprinkled her sons with this, and then shot arrows of spruce and pine over them to restore them to consciousness.

The Enemyway has never been a ceremony to prepare for war, as many people think, even in the days of long ago, but rather it is to rid the patient from the effects of any "enemy." It is a ritual conducted for persons who are disposed to weakness or fainting, often attributed to the sight of blood, or from witnessing sudden or violent death, or from dreams of the same sort. Therefore, the symptoms are chiefly psychological. An "enemy" is a foreigner, whether he be white or of any other race, or even Indians of other tribes, and the purpose of the ceremony is to drive away the "ghosts" of such enemies. This has grown to be hypothetical, and the "ghosts" may be the effect that any foreigner has had on a Navaho. The slaying of the ghost is now interpreted as ridding a person from foreign influence. Following both World War II and the Korean War, in which many young Navaho served in the Armed Forces, there were countless ceremonies held on the return of these veterans to rid them of the effects of all they had experienced.

As the enemy is to be "fought," a site is chosen at some distance from the patient's hogan where a temporary ceremonial hogan is erected. Since Enemyway is a summer ceremony, this may be a brush shelter, roofed over with cut boughs. Then the patient, who must secure the services of a "scalper," sends a messenger out on horseback after the enemy's scalp. Usually the scalper is an older man, one who has seen blood in some sort of combat. Certain men who qualify for this position keep the necessary trophies hidden away for this special use. These trophies may be a real scalp from long ago, or locks of hair, or bits of clothing from an enemy. In order to signify his mission, the scalper carries the trophy on a stick, holding it out in front of him, so that no one will come too close to him. When he reaches the patient's hogan he is shown where the scalp is to be buried, usually a spot a short distance east of the ceremonial hogan where the scalp is deposited and stones are placed over it.

The most important feature of the Enemyway is the Rattle Stick. As the trimming of this symbol must be performed by a singer who knows the songs of the ceremony, the proper individual must be sought. Also, someone to be the Stick Receiver must be found, someone who knows the rest of the ceremonial and who lives some distance away, perhaps eight or ten miles.

When the singer (the stick decorator) arrives at the appointed time, he asks for an earthen jar which will become the pot drum of the ceremony and whose function when beaten is to drive the ghosts into the ground. The person who brings the pot to the singer pours water into it, first from the East, then the South, West, and North, and finally from above. Then a piece of buckskin is fitted over the rim of the jar and held in place by thongs. Often pots are kept for this specific purpose. When the cover is in place, holes are punched into it resembling eyes and mouth. The cover becomes moist and taut so that it will produce a hollow sound when beaten. Rather than the usual drum stick, a tapper is made of a native shrub, with one end bent into a loop. Both the drum and the tapper are dedicated to the ceremony by prayers and song. This dedication takes place under a brush shelter which has been erected just east of the ceremonial hogan. Here for the first time the singer sings the important Four First Songs, then all those present join in singing other songs.

At sunrise the next day the singer selects someone to go for the Stick, which must be a piece of cedar or juniper, about eighteen inches long with no flaws or branches. The messenger, who usually goes on horseback, notes which side of his selected branch faces to the East before he cuts it from the tree, then, after sprinkling some sacred corn pollen at the base of the tree, he returns to the ceremonial hogan carrying the Stick in a specified manner covered with a cloth. As he approaches, the people in the hogan prepare the ceremonial basket, making a small circle of pollen in it as the messenger enters.

To prepare the Stick with its significant symbols, the singer directs someone to carve the designs with an arrowhead on the sides of the Stick. On the east side he carves a bow, being careful to move the arrowhead in the right direction, from left to right. On the opposite side a queue is carved, again in the right direction, and in both carvings a small opening (the Spirit Path) is left at the end. The symbolic queue stems from the origin legend, for it is said that Changing Woman first tied her hair in a queue before the Twins were born. All Navaho women, and many men, still style their hair in this "chongo." The bow is symbolic of Changing Woman's shooting the arrows over the Twins.

Over the years and at different places, Betsy and I have seen most of this ceremony. But in 1951, while we were visiting at Wide Ruins, we went with Mrs. Lippincott to see the trimming of the Rattle Stick. When we entered the hogan, the singer was about to commence this phase of the ritual. After walking clockwise around the center, we took our places on the north side of the hogan. Here indeed was a lovely scene, for this brush hogan roof was letting the sunlight filter through onto the dark-skinned faces, accenting the color of their head bands and scarfs as they watched the singer examining the carvings just completed on the Stick, while he sang again the Four First Songs in a subdued voice. Then he applied a mixture of burnt herbs and tallow to the surface of the Stick. First he used a black tallow, then some red, while he sang the proper songs. The patient's face was also daubed with the tallow, black on his chin, red on the rest of his face, but the singer was careful to save the proper amount to send to the Stick Receiver later in the day. Beside the singer was a small pile of herbs—sage, grama grass, and other plants—from which he selected certain pieces to be bound onto the Stick together with a turkey feather. Then he added two small eagle feathers and some deer hooves,

*Bringing in the stick to be trimmed.*

tying them all to the Rattle Stick. While the singer was still quietly singing the proper songs, the women came forth to add further trimmings—pieces of ribbon, bits of yarn, usually red, and, from those who still had some, strips of bayeta—all of which were added to the Stick by means of slip knots. When this was finished, the patient took the Stick, and, holding it with the bow design facing the East, walked out of the hogan where his assistants were holding his horse, saddled and ready for the race to the Stick Receiver's camp some ten miles away. We watched the group of racing horsemen as soon as we were able to leave the hogan.

As we knew where the Receiver's camp was, while the horsemen were racing across the country we drove around by the road, arriving just in time to see them coming into the camp. The Stick Receiver stood before his hogan as the riders approached and dismounted. The patient first handed the Receiver the red and black tallow; then holding the Rattle Stick he pointed it first to the Receiver's feet, then brought it upward, circling his head, and, finally placed it in the Receiver's left hand. The Receiver in turn placed the Stick in a basket to inspect the designs and, deciding that they were properly made, accepted the Stick by bringing the designs close to his mouth, and inhaling deeply, indicating his acceptance. Taking the trimmings from the Rattle Stick, he distributed them among the people of his camp; then with the tallow

*The women go to the shelter..*

*Racing off with the Rattle Stick.*

*Bread making at a Squaw Dance.*

*The cook shelter for the Enemyway.*

brought by the patient he painted the faces of those nearby, and sprayed them with the herb mixture. The Receiver's party also prepared a pot drum. The Stick Receiver was now in complete charge of the ceremony. We did not stay beyond this point at this particular ceremony, but we knew that there would now be a rest period and the eating of a meal.

When the ritual is resumed toward evening, the Receiver selects an unmarried girl to be the custodian of the Stick, and, following her, both parties move to the dance ground where, as at the first site, the Four First Songs are sung over the pot drum as it is tapped. Following this, the Indians group themselves around the drummer, and with a swaying motion sing a great variety of songs. The dancing commences as each girl chooses a man, and, standing behind him, moves him in a circle several times, then reverses the motion. If a man wishes to be released, he must pay his partner before she will let him go. Much amusement is derived from this phase of the dance. Toward dawn, the Receiver again takes the Stick and standing in the midst of the circle awaits the daylight, when he takes it inside his hogan while both groups join to feed the entire assembly, which may have grown large during the night.

The following morning, relatives and friends of the Receiver bring small gifts of tobacco, food, money, cloth, and other items, heaping them on a blanket laid out for the purpose just inside the hogan. The members of the patient's group gathered outside to serenade the Receiver. The leader once more sings the Four First Songs at the entrance while the drum is

*Gathering for the dance.*

beaten, then other songs continue. The Receiver throws the gifts out of the smoke hole in the roof of the hogan, regardless of who may catch them. This is the only Navaho ceremony where an exchange of gifts takes place. It is considered symbolic of appreciation that the earth's productivity has been restored.

Following the throwing of the gifts, the patient and his party return to their own hogan, being very careful to retrace their own hoof prints. As each rider reaches the original ceremonial hogan he must once more circle the fire in the proper direction. Preparations then go forward for the next day, when the Stick Receiver and his party will arrive at the original site. more colored tallow is prepared, more herbs are burnt, and the spray solution is mixed for the final ritual.

In the evening of the second night at the Receiver's camp, the Four First Songs are repeated and the dance continues as on the night before.

At dawn the next morning, the Stick Decorator at the first site prepares for the ceremonies. The patient and his family wash their hair in yucca suds and prepare for the emesis to follow. This cleansing both within and without symbolizes the removal of any traces of the effects of the "enemy ghost."

Fairly early in the morning of this last day, the gathering of people at the Receiver's camp mount their horses and start for the patient's hogan. The same unmarried girl carries the Stick, and a man brings the pot drum. As they near their destination a group of horsemen at the patient's hogan go forth to meet the Receiver's party, discharging their guns as they go, and the two groups meet in a mock battle. Then they all dash around the hogan four times, chasing one another in a wide circle. The Receiver's party make a camp a short distance away while the women from the cook shelter immediately bring them food.

After the meal and a short rest, the pot drum is again tapped at the entrance of the ceremonial hogan as another group of serenaders gather to sing the Four First Songs once more, while friends and relatives of the patient enter the hogan to place gifts for distribution. Those from the Receiver's camp, who caught the thrown gifts the day before, now enter with new exchange gifts. Again these are thrown out of the smoke hole to be gathered or caught by those who are standing around the hogan.

Now the patient is blackened in preparation for the "killing of the scalp." Both men and women may join in this final part of the ceremony, though the patient's wife may ask someone to substitute for her. The significance of the blackening again refers to the original legend, in which Monster Slayer was blackened so that Yeitso could not see him. The men strip to a G string and their entire bodies are blackened.

With Mrs. Lippincott, Betsy and I watched this last part of the ceremony in 1951, as we had earlier watched its beginning. The wife of the patient and a group of women entered the shelter opposite the ceremonial hogan, where we were invited to join the participants. Then we all knelt down while the women held a blanket over the wife as she changed her dress and bared her shoulders so that she too might be blackened. We saw, out of the corners of our eyes, the blackened figure of the patient emerging from the hogan, his small son beside him. In his hand he carried a crow bill, symbolic of the scavenger, as he walked toward the buried scalp. Soon we heard the shot fired to kill the enemy ghost, following which the patient made jabbing motions with the crow's bill, and scattered ashes of the "slain enemy." The ceremony was over and all participants retired to rest and, later, to prepare the big feast in the evening prior to the final dance that night.

Some differences exist in the Enemyway as performed by different singers, and some special rites may be added, but fundamentally this is the story of the most frequently given ceremony among the Navaho. We have found that relatively few non-Indian people have seen the colorful, reverent trimming of the Rattle Stick, and the many daytime rituals of the Enemyway.

### *The Elements*

The Navaho personify the elements: the winds, lightning, thunder, fog, mist, rain. Of all these, only rain has duality, the "He" rain and the "She" rain. The "He" rain is the violent thunderstorm that drives the seeds into the earth; the "She" rain is the gentle rain that nurtures the soil and brings forth the crops. The rainbow is considered the path of the Yei, and is depicted in many of the sand paintings. Because much damage can come from the elements, these divinities are invoked by prayer and song with prayer sticks and sacrifices, so that no harm will come to the People.

For centuries the Navaho People have led the outdoor life. Their hogans, expertly designed to withstand the elements, provide shelter at night and during storms, but sometimes the Indians are caught away from home by spring duststorms, summer thunderstorms, or winter snowstorms. One needs to experience such as these, alone, out in those great desert reaches when the wind, rain, or snow sweeps the country with gigantic force, to understand why the Navaho have always felt the power of the elements, and have offered a prayer with a song.

The Navaho have myths concerning the stars and have considerable knowledge and awareness of constellations and period phenomena. Fire God, according to the legend, created the stars, giving each its proper name as he took them from his pouch and threw them into the sky, scattering the remnants to form the Milky Way. There is another legend, in which Coyote stole the Fire God's pouch and, after placing his own star in the southern sky, threw all the rest far up into the heavens, which accounts for the many unnamed stars.

A writer in the book *An Ethnological Dictionary of the Navajo Language* says, ". . . the origin and motive of each chant is based upon its own peculiar legend. And it must be a cause for regret that very

*The "He" rain.*

few singers now living in the tribe are conversant with the chant legends, and, as a consequence, many chants are becoming extinct." Since this was written, in 1910, many younger Navaho have become interested in preserving their past, and a Department of Archives has been established at Window Rock. Already there is the nucleus of a museum with a resident historian, and eventually young Navaho children will have this additional source of knowledge of their ancestral heritage.

In the long prayer from the Night Chant, there is a portion addressed to the mythological Thunder Bird, with reference to its flight. The bird is spoken of as a male divinity who is supposed to live at Tsegi.

> With the far darkness made of the he-rain
> over your head, come to us soaring
> With the far darkness made of the she-rain
> over your head, come to us soaring
> With the zig zag lightning flung out on high
> over your head, come to us soaring
> With the rainbow hanging high
> over your head, come to us soaring.[1]

[1] Dr. Washington Matthews, *Navaho Legends*, pp. 273–275.

*The "She" rain.*

*The Nightway*

Of all the long ceremonials, the one most frequently given is the Nightway, or Yeibichai. This nine-day ceremony is very complex, containing much ritualistic procedure which must be carried out in minute detail and in exactly the prescribed order. It begins in the evening of the first day when the medicine man, or chanter, arrives at the selected site. His first act is to apply the Yeibichai talisman to the patient by successively placing it about the patient's waist, his shoulders, his neck, and his head. This talisman is made of four carefuly selected pieces of willow, each eighteen inches long, attached to each other with woolen strings, so that they may be spread out into an open rectangle and folded up again. A chanter receives his talisman from his preceptor and may keep it for life, transmitting it eventually to his pupil.

To describe in detail this entire ceremony would take many pages and has been done magnificently by Dr. Washington Matthews.[2] It has been my good fortune to see parts of the first eight days, and Betsy and

[2] See the Bibliography.

*Sand painting*
*at a Yeibichai Ceremony.*

I have seen the ninth day and night several times. The Nightway, perhaps more than any other ceremony, contains the greatest amount of minute detail in the preparation of the many prayersticks, the costumes, and the masks (for there are many impersonators of the Yei), and in the making of five beautiful sand paintings.

The chanter consecrates the ceremonial hogan by sprinkling sacred meal as he moves clockwise around the interior of the hogan. If the patient is a man, he uses white meal, if a woman, yellow. This consecration is repeated on the fourth night, the night of the vigil of the gods. All during the day there is much preparation for the vigil when the impersonators keep watch over their masks and other objects as they sing and pray the whole night through. The principal character of the Yeibichai is Talking God (Hastseyalte), the creator of the ceremonies, who utters his peculiar cry, "Wu, hu, hu, hu," at the important moments to announce that all has been done correctly.

Usually only the patient and his family are present for the first eight days of the ceremony, with the medicine man and his helpers, but on the ninth day visitors arrive to participate in the final rites. As with the Mountainway, the daytime of the last day is filled with preparation for the night ceremony. An area before the hogan is cleared for the dancers. A wood pile is prepared, and as the people arrive each family finds a place along the side of the clearing. An arbor of green branches is erected at the far end where the impersonators will put on their masks. All during the day and evening, ritual goes on inside the ceremonial hogan.

Shortly before the night ceremony begins, four great fires are lighted. Inside the hogan the dancers are being prepared: their bodies are painted with a white clay, and the costumes are put on. The masks, the wands of spruce, and the fox skins have previously been placed in the arbor along its northern side. Talking God masks and dresses in the hogan and when all is ready he gives his cry to clear the dance ground. Then the four impersonators, wrapped in blankets, precede Talking God and the chanter as they go to the arbor to put on their masks. While wearing the masks no impersonator must ever speak—only Talking God utters his special cry. The dancers' costumes consist of short kilts, made of some special material, often hand-woven, silver belts from which the fox skins hang from the back, long hand-knit stockings, necklaces, and the plumed masks with spruce-twig collars attached. Each dancer carries a gourd rattle in his right hand, a wand of spruce in his left. Talking God wears his special mask and collar, is clothed in his deerskin robe, and carries a fawn-skin bag in one hand. As the dancers leave the arbor the medicine man leads, with Talking God and the four impersonators following. The chanter utters the benediction, scattering pollen as the group crosses the dance ground to the hogan. As they approach, the dancers quietly shake their rattles, singing as they walk. The patient comes out of the hogan carrying a ceremonial basket containing sacred meal, sometimes with four special prayersticks on top. While the chanter says a prayer over the meal, the four Yei keep up a constant motion of their feet. After this prayer, the chanter assists the patient, who advances to sprinkle the sacred meal over each of the Yei in turn. Taking a large pinch, the patient lets some fall first on the right hand of each Yei, then sprinkles the meal up the right arm, over the top of the forehead, and down the left arm, and drops what is left in the palm of the left hand, the patient using his right hand while he carries the basket on his left arm. Then the patient and the chanter resume their positions in front of the hogan door, facing to the East. The Chanter now recites the long prayer to each of the Yei, the patient repeating after him, verse by verse. These prayers are similar except in mentioning certain attributes of each Yei. The prayer ends:

> In Beauty (happily) I walk
> With Beauty before me I walk
> With Beauty behind me I walk
> With Beauty above me I walk
> With Beauty all around me I walk
> It is finished in Beauty.
>
> [Repeated four times]

This oft-quoted poem, impressive as it is, is far from an adequate translation, for there seems to be no English word to convey the idea of the Navaho concept of "in harmony with." Navaho words, of course fit into the song, while an English translation is difficult to adapt. Gladys Reichard has given the following:

*Wood for the bonfires.*

*The dance ground for the Nightway.*

May there be happiness
May there be success
May there be good health
May there be well being.

The entire song builds up to the comprehensive idea of being in harmony with the universe.

When the prayer is ended, the patient follows the chanter as they pass eastward down the north side of the line and back, scattering more meal as they pass. The patient places the basket near the hogan door, the chanter sitting to his left, as they both face to the East, looking at the dancers. All the spectators now become silent and attentive, waiting for the sacred song. Talking God, who has been standing north of the line of dancers facing the South, turns and rushes to the East, uttering his cry, and holds up his bag as a signal to the four Yei. They at once advance their left feet, bending their bodies to the right, and, shaking their rattles, they dip them with a long sweep of their arms, as if scooping up water, bringing them up to their mouths. Then Talking God rushes to the West and repeats his action while the dancers face

(OPPOSITE AND BELOW) *Awaiting the night ceremonial.*

the West and repeat theirs, then face East again, always turning clockwise. Talking God stamps his feet twice as a signal, and the Yei commence the dance step. This is all done four times before the song begins. First facing the East, then the West, the dancers make eight changes of direction during the song. Because the song is the most important part of the entire ceremony, it has been thoroughly rehearsed in private. Should there be a single mistake or a misplaced word, the ceremony terminates immediately and the entire nine-day ritual is considered valueless.

The corn comes up, the rain descends
The corn plant comes therewith,
The rain descends, the corn comes up
The child-rain comes therewith.

The corn comes up, the rain descends
Vegetation comes herewith
The rain descends, the corn comes up
The pollen comes herewith.

[Continued with many verses]

Talking God may be standing still or walking up

*The long prayer*
*at the Nightway.*

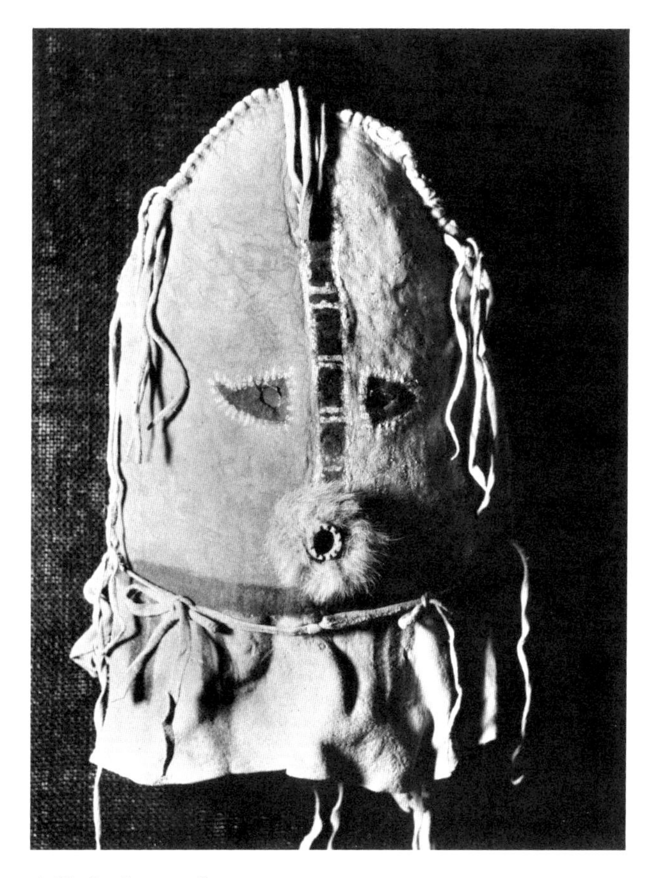

*A Yeibichai mask.*

and down but at the end of each stanza he gives his cry to indicate that he has detected no error. When the song is finished, the singers are facing the West. They turn to the East and, as Talking God leads, they start for the arbor, at first shaking their rattles, then walking in silence. In the arbor they take off their masks and lay them with their rattles along the north side. After the masks are off the impersonators may talk. They return to the hogan without formality, where they pray, wash the paint off their bodies, and resume ordinary dress.

Following an interval, the long Yeibichai dance begins, usually with twelve dancers taking part. There will be six Yebaka (male) dancers and six Yebaad (female) dancers, though the latter usually are impersonated by youths or small men. Both the Yebaka and the Yebaad are dressed alike with the exception of the masks, those of the Yebaad being domino masks.

Again the chanter leads them from the arbor with Talking God following him, then the twelve dancers, while Tenenili, the rain god, and Fringe Mouth, the clown, bring up the rear. They approach the hogan and commence their dance with songs of many verses and many repetitions. To relieve the monotony throughout the rest of the night, the clown does acts of simple buffoonery, Talking God sometimes joining him. Slowly, with constant rhythm, the dance continues, variations being largely in the words of the songs.

Just as the dawn breaks, everyone, visitors and performers alike, stand facing the East as the Prayer to the Dawn is repeated. All inhale the dawn in prayer that its purity and strength may enter into them. When the prayer is ended the Bluebird song is heard, for to the Navaho, too, the bluebird is the symbol of happiness and heralds the break of day.

> Just at daylight bluebird calls.
> The bluebird has a voice
> His voice melodious that flows in gladness
> Bluebird calls. Bluebird calls.[3]

To observe such a ceremonial as the Nightway is an experience long to be remembered. Listening to the high-pitched voices, watching the dancers, observing the spectators who have come to take part in the ritual, feeling the assembled reverence as the Prayer to the Dawn is sung in the chill, clear Southwestern air, makes one realize the strength and beauty to be derived from closeness to the elements. Here is something vital, something real.

[3] Translation by Frances E. Watkins, Southwest Museum, Highland Park, Los Angeles, California.

# EPILOGUE

Among the many Navaho people of the Red Rock area with whom Betsy worked, one family, near neighbors, were special friends. Francis Nakai and his wife (we never have known what her name is, so we have always called her "Mrs. Francis") lived in a small frame house directly south of Betsy's quarters, perhaps a quarter of a mile away. During the early years of Betsy's association with them, Francis was one of the outstanding men in the area, a good farmer and provider for his family. They had two sons, Juan and Louis, boys of perhaps eight and twelve when we first knew them. Mrs. Francis was one of Betsy's frequent visitors. She would come, sit for a while, drink a cup of coffee, but, as she spoke no English, conversation was very limited. She had great charm, however, and whenever I paid Betsy a visit I saw her frequently. It was she whom we took to Santa Fe to see the blankets in the Indian Arts Fund Collection, and who dined with us at our friend's birthday party.

Over the years when we were away from New Mexico and Arizona, we often had letters from Francis, sending us news of the people at Red Rock, and always asking when we were coming back to see them. It was seventeen years before we saw them again, and we found many changes. Still living in the same little house, they then had two daughters, much younger than the boys we had first known. The oldest son had been killed in the European theatre of World War II, and almost the only object in the room in which we were sitting was the flag that had been over the boy's coffin at the time of his burial in France. Both Francis and his wife seemed dejected and we were distressed by the change. A year or so later, we saw them again.

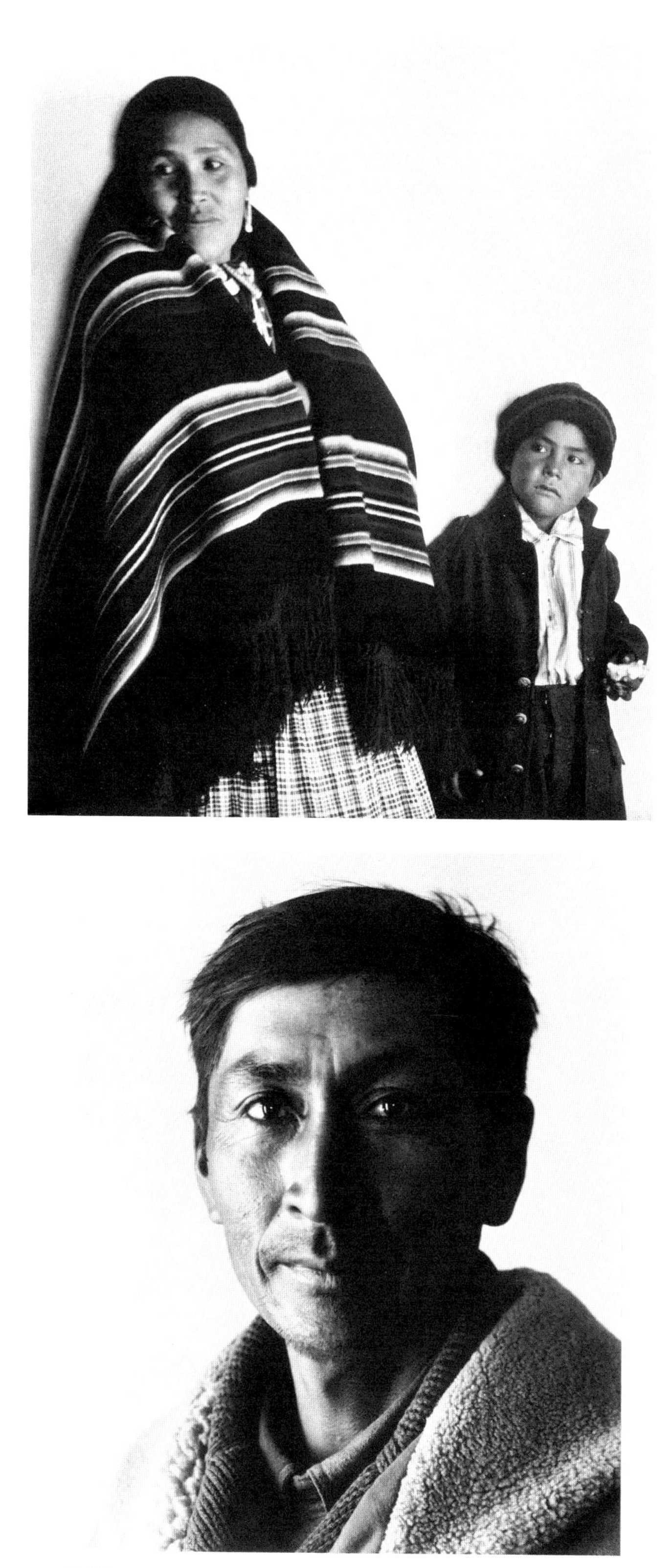

They had moved to the community of Shiprock where Francis had some sort of job with the Indian Agency. We found that alcohol was the problem. After that we saw them every few years and always matters seemed to be a little worse. Then in 1962 we were at the Shiprock Fair and found them down by the river, where Francis was selling a large crop of melons he had raised. They both looked and seemed much more like their old selves, and we felt hopeful that the problem was well in hand; from talking to others later, we found indeed that it was.

In the fall of 1964 we drove into Shiprock over the new highway from Monument Valley. Enquiring for our old friends at Charles Dickens' Trading Post, we learned that Francis had died from pneumonia the previous winter, and that Mrs. Francis had moved back to Red Rock. We drove out to see her, and there we found her back in the same little frame house with her two daughters and their babies. Mrs. Francis burst into tears when she saw us and it took Betsy quite a while to quiet and comfort her. We talked to the two daughters, giving them some fruit we had brought, and, when it was time for us to go, Mrs. Francis took my hand and put into it a beautiful hand-woven belt she had recently made. As we drove away, Betsy had them all smiling and happy.

But this must have been a very nostalgic visit for Betsy. We looked at the familiar landscape, finding many changes. The old concrete hospital building that had been Betsy's home and where she had held her clinic had been completely removed, not a trace was left. Other buildings too were gone, one, the old barn by the trading post. But there were some signs of progress, for up the road toward the mountains was a fine new school. Trees had been planted around it which were already of some size. Though she said nothing, I was sure that Betsy's mind was filled with thoughts of her many friends and the work she had done during those years of her nursing service here at Red Rock, a service meaning more to her than anything she had ever done. We have seen some eight or ten families of her old friends during the past ten or twelve years, most of them former patients, and from each Betsy received a heart-warming welcome. As we have found so often, once an Indian has learned to trust a person, the bond is lasting.

We drove quietly back over the old familiar road, passing Shiprock, eternal and beautiful as it cast its

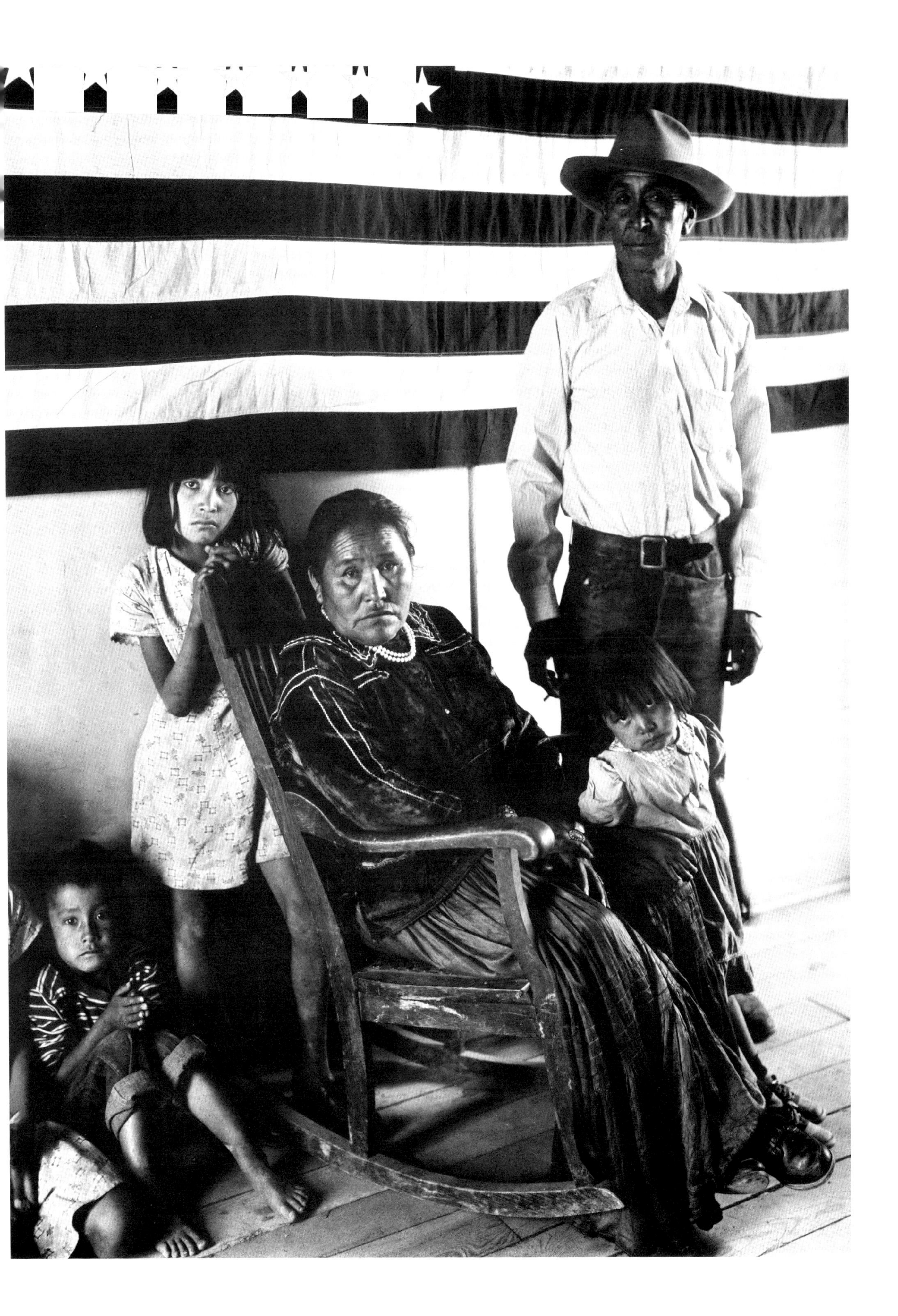

long shadow over the desert floor in the late afternoon light, filling us with tranquillity and peace.

While the year 1968 will commemorate the centennial anniversary of the end of the Navaho banishment to Bosque Redondo, one remembers the return of the Dinéh to the land that was their home, after those four devastating years, bereft of all possessions and with the taste of defeat still bitter in their memories as they turned to the task of rebuilding their lives. For a time there was apathy among many who felt frustrated in returning to their old ways and knew not how to adjust to the new, but slowly they did adjust, and now for more than two decades they have marched steadfastly along the road we call modern civilization.

A new day has arrived for the young Navaho as they adapt themselves to the white man's way. Many are absorbing this life with eagerness, choosing those occupations sympathetic to their inclinations; some are simply leading a new kind of life, while many still continue their traditional way. Most young Navaho face this great change with sureness and confidence.

A short time ago, as I was driving from Gallup to Shiprock, I overtook a young couple walking along the highway. They had been to the Window Rock Fair, and after I picked them up to give them a lift we dropped into easy conversation. We drove more than thirty miles before the young man asked me to stop. We were in the empty desert country which extends for miles along this highway and there was not even one hogan in sight. As I watched them walk away, finally melting into the landscape, I thought of the tremendous changes that have come to such young people as these. There are many thousands of young Navaho who are pushing aside the traditional ways taught by their parents, wanting to partake fully of non-Indian culture. But there are also many, both young and old, who are concerned about this rejection of the past and who are trying to preserve the ways of their people.

Many who know the Navaho well think that the great days of ceremonialism are past. Possibly this is true, but I cannot believe that the old ways will really be lost. Another generation will want to know all those things that their grandparents can tell them, and I am sure that there will always be some who can do so, and that a new interest in their traditional past will come. Who can say whether there will or will not be a great revival? We can but hope that those essential qualities that are the birthright of the Dinéh will never be lost. Song and singing are the very essence of Navaho being, and as long as the Navaho keep singing, their tradition will endure.

# APPENDICES

# BIBLIOGRAPHY

# INDEX

# APPENDICES

## CHRONOLOGY

*Some important dates in Navaho history:*

1550 plus or minus 30 years—Earliest evidence of Navaho to date [1963].

1626—First mention of Navaho People by Spanish Explorers.

1712—Earliest known Navaho date in Canyon de Chelly.

1846—Mexican War. Entry of General Kearney into Santa Fe.

1846–1847—Treaty of Bear Springs.

1846–1863—The military period.

1849—The Washington Expedition.

1861—Abandonment of Fort Defiance as troops leave for Civil War.

1864—Defeat of Navaho by Colonel Kit Carson.

1864–1868—Exile to Fort Sumner.

1868—Signing of treaty at Fort Sumner. Establishment of reservation (3,328,000 acres).

1869—First trading post at Fort Defiance.

1871—Beginning of wool trade.

1874—Beginning of trade with Mormons.

1876—First licensed trader (other than government post at Fort Defiance), Thomas V. Keam.

1878—Establishment of Hubbell Trading Post at Ganado.

1882—Creation of Hopi Reservation.

1884—Lee's Ferry on the Colorado River.

1885—Influx of non-Indian sheepmen in Checkerboard Area.

1886—First water development appropriation under President Cleveland.

1887—Land and water difficulties in Checkerboard and San Juan River areas. Arrival of first non-Indian prospectors on reservation. Passage of compulsory school act.

1890—Sam E. Day Post at Chinle. Beginning of Fred Harvey Company interest in Navaho products.

1900—Addition of 1,750,000 acres to the western reservation.

1907—Addition by President Roosevelt of Pueblo Bonito Reservation area to the eastern boundary of the reservation.

1911—Rescinding by President Taft of Pueblo Bonito Reservation; restored to public domain.

1916—Grazing Homestead Act.

1921—Discovery of oil in Shiprock area.

1922—Establishment of first Navaho Business Council.

1923—Election of first Tribal Council.

1927—Establishment of Chapter by John Hunter of Leupp Agency.

1930–1931—Addition by Congress of the Paiute and Aneth Extension in Utah to the reservation.

1931—Increase of Tribal Council to seventy-four delegates.

1934—Addition by Arizona Boundary Bill of 792,366 acres to western reservation. Unification of Navaho agencies into one, established at Window Rock.

1938—Establishment of voting registration and ballots with pictures of candidates.

1940—Establishment of Department of Resources.

1950—Discovery of uranium ore on reservation.

1953—Establishment of Education Scholarship Fund. Establishment of Navaho Police Force. Repeal of prohibition law for Indians in New Mexico.

1954—Repeal of prohibition law for Indians in Arizona.

1956—Beginning of construction of Glen Canyon Dam.

1957—Discovery of new oil fields in Four Corners Area.

1960—Exchange of land occupied by Glen Canyon Dam area for McCracken Mesa Area in San Juan County, Utah. Total area occupied by Navaho people approximately 16,000,000 acres.

1963—Completion of Navajo Reservoir Dam. Completion of Glen Canyon Dam.

## NAVAHO PRONUNCIATION GUIDE

*Simplified phonetic vowel symbols:*

*ah*: for *a* as in *father*
*ay*, as in *say*
*aye*, as in *aye*
*ee*, as in *seen*
*eh*: for *e* as in *bet*
*gh*: for *g* as in *go*
*i*, as in *sip*
*ł*: for *lth*
*oh*: for *o* as in *so*
*zh*: for *s* as in *pleasure*

Ahkeah (Ah-KEE-ah)
Atsidi Sani (Ah-TSI-dee SAH-nee)
Beclabito (Bi-CLAH-bi-toh)
Begay (Be-GAY)
Bekéya (Bi-KAY-yah)
Bekiss (Bi-kiss)
Beta-ta-kin (Beh-TAH-tah-kin)
Chee (Chee)
Chetro Ketl (Chehtro Kettle)
Chinle (Chin-LEE)
Ch'óół'í'í (CHOHL-ee-ee)
Chuska (CHUHS-kah)
Coconino (Koh-koh-NEE-noh)
de Chelly (de SHAY)
Desha Chischillige (DAY-shah Chish-CHIL-i-gee)
Dibéntsaa (Di-BEH-n-tsah)
Dinéh (di-NEH)
Doko'oosłííd (Doh-koh-ohs LTHEED)
Dził na'oodiłii (Dzilth NAH-oh-dilth-ee)
Ha-So-De (Hoh-soh-deh)
Hastseyalte (Hahsh-chay-YALTH-tee-ee)
hogan (HOH-gahn)
Hopi (HOH-pee)
Hosteen Nez (Has-teen NEHZ)
Hozhoji (hoh-ZHON-jee)
Kayenta (Kay-YEHN-tah)
ketoh (KAY-toh)
Kiis'aanii (Kees-AH-nee)
Lukachukai (LUH-kah-CHUH-kaye)
Naatsis'áán (Nah-tsis-AHN)
Nadene (NAH-deh-neh)
Najah (NAH-zhah)
Nakai Tsosi (NAH-kaye TSOH-see)
Navaho (NAH-vah-hoh)
Sanostee (Sah-NAHS-tee)
Shonto (SHAHN-toh)
Sisnaajiní (SIS-nah-ji-nee)
Tahoma (Tah-HOH-mah)
Tauglechee (TAH-gl-chee)
Toadlena (Toh-ah-DLEE-nah)
Tohatchi (TOH-ha-chee)
Tseghi (TSAY-ghee)
Tsihnajinnie (TSI-nah-ji-nee)
Tsoodził (TSHO-dzilth)
Wauneka (Waw-NEE-kah)
Yebaad (YAY-ee-bah-ahd)
Yebaka (YAY-ee-bah-kaha)
Yei (YAY-ee)
Yeitso (YAY-ee-tsoh)

# BIBLIOGRAPHY

*A partial list of authoritative books on the Navaho People*


Adair, John. *The Navajo and Pueblo Silversmiths.* Norman: University of Oklahoma Press, 1944.

Amsden, Charles Avery. *Navaho Weaving.* Santa Ana, California: Fine Arts Press, 1934.

Coolidge, Dane, and Mary R. Coolidge. *The Navajo Indians,* New York: Houghton Mifflin Co., 1930.

DeHarport, David L. "Origin of the Name, Cañon del Muerto," *El Palacio,* 67, No. 3 (June, 1960), 95.

Franciscan Fathers, The. *An Ethnologic Dictionary.* Saint Michael's Mission, Arizona: Saint Michael's Press, 1910.

Greever, William S. *Arid Domain: The Santa Fe Railroad and Its Western Land Grants.* Palo Alto, California: Stanford University Press, 1954.

Haile, Father Berard. *The Navaho Fire Dance.* Saint Michael's Mission, Arizona: Saint Michael's Press, 1946.

———. *The Navaho War Dance.* Saint Michael's Mission, Arizona: Saint Michael's Press, 1946.

Hill, W. W. "The Hand Tremblers," *El Palacio,* 38 (March–April, 1935), 65.

James, George Wharton. *Indian Blankets and Their Makers.* New York: Tudor Publ. Co., 1937.

Jones, Courtney R. "Spindle Spinning: Navajo Style," *Plateau,* 18, No. 3 (January, 1946), 43–51.

Kluckhohn, Clyde, and Dorothea Leighton. *The Navaho.* Garden City, N. Y.: Anchor Books, Doubleday & Co., 1962.

Leighton, Alexander H., and Dorothea C. Leighton. *The Navaho Door.* Cambridge, Mass.: Harvard University Press, 1944.

MacNeish, "The Origins of New World Civilization," *Scientific American,* 211, No. 5 (November, 1964), 29–37.

McNitt, Frank. *The Indian Traders.* Norman: University of Oklahoma Press, 1962.

———. *Richard Wetherill: Anasazi.* Albuquerque: University of New Mexico Press, 1957.

Matthews, Washington. *Basket Making.* Washington, D. C.: Bureau of American Ethnology, 1902.

———. *Navaho Legends.* Memoir Series, Vol. V. American Folk-Lore Society, 1897.

———. *Navaho Silversmithing.* Washington, D. C.: Bureau of American Ethnology, 1880–1881.

———. *The Night Chant.* Memoirs of the American Museum of Natural History, Vol. VI. New York: 1902.

———. *The Night Chant.* Washington, D. C.: Bureau of American Ethnology, 1884.

Mitchell, Emerson Blackhorse, and T. D. Allen. *Miracle Hill: The Story of a Navaho Boy.* Norman: University of Oklahoma Press, 1967.

*Navajo Yearbook,* compiled by Robert W. Young. Window Rock, Arizona: Navajo Agency, 1961.

Newcomb, Franc Johnson. *Hosteen Klah.* Norman: University of Oklahoma Press, 1964.

———. *Navaho Folk Tales.* Santa Fe: Museum of Navaho Ceremonial Art, 1967.

———. *Navajo Omens and Taboos.* Santa Fe: Rydal Press, 1940.

O'Bryan, Aileen. *The Diné: Origin Myths of the Navaho Indians.* Smithsonian Institution. Bureau of American Ethnology. Bulletin 163. 1956.

Reichard, Gladys A. *Navajo Shepherd and Weaver.* New York: J. J. Augustin, 1936.

———. *Spider Woman.* New York: The Macmillan Co., 1934.

Schevill, Margaret Erwin. *Beautiful on the Earth.* Santa Fe: Hazel Dries Editions, 1947.

Simpson, Lt. James H. *Navaho Expedition,* edited and annotated by Frank McNitt. Norman: University of Oklahoma Press, 1964.

Tschopik, Harry, Jr. "Navaho Pottery Making," *Papers of the Peabody Museum of Archaeology and Ethnology*, 17, No. 1. (1941), 7–79.

Van Valkenburgh, Richard F. *A Brief History of the Navaho People.* Window Rock, Arizona: U. S. Department of the Interior, 1946.

———. *Diné Bekéyah.* Window Rock, Arizona: U. S. Department of the Interior, 1941.

———. *Sacred Places and Shrines of the Navaho.* Window Rock, Arizona: U. S. Department of the Interior, 1938.

Waters, Frank. *Masked Gods: Navaho and Pueblo Ceremonialism.* Albuquerque: University of New Mexico Press, 1950.

Wyman, Leland C. *Navaho Sand Paintings: The Huckel Collection.* Colorado Springs: The Taylor Museum of the Colorado Springs Fine Arts Center, 1960.

# INDEX